NTSB/RAR-13/02
PB2013-107679
Notation 8431B
Adopted June 18, 2013

Railroad Accident Report

Head-On Collision of Two Union Pacific
Railroad Freight Trains Near
Goodwell, Oklahoma
June 24, 2012

**National
Transportation
Safety Board**

490 L'Enfant Plaza, SW
Washington, DC 20594

National Transportation Safety Board. 2013. *Head-On Collision of Two Union Pacific Railroad Freight Trains Near Goodwell, Oklahoma, June 24, 2012.* Railroad Accident Report NTSB/RAR-13/02. Washington, DC.

Abstract: On Sunday, June 24, 2012, at 10:02 a.m. central daylight time, eastbound Union Pacific Railroad (UP) freight train ZLAAH 22 and westbound UP freight train AAMMLX 22 collided head-on while operating on straight track on the UP Pratt subdivision near Goodwell, Oklahoma. The collision derailed 3 locomotives and 24 cars of the eastbound train and 2 locomotives and 8 cars of the westbound train. The engineer and the conductor of the eastbound train and the engineer of the westbound train were killed. The conductor of the westbound train jumped to safety. During the collision and derailment, several fuel tanks from the derailed locomotives ruptured, releasing diesel fuel that ignited and burned. Damage was estimated at $14.8 million.

Safety issues identified in this investigation were the actions and responsibilities of the train crews, the medical examination process for railroad engineer certification, the survivability of event recorder data, and the need for implementation of positive train control. The National Transportation Safety Board makes safety recommendations to the Federal Railroad Administration, the Brotherhood of Locomotive Engineers and Trainmen, the United Transportation Union, all Class I Railroads, the Union Pacific Railroad, and all railroads subject to the positive train control provisions of the Rail Safety Improvement Act of 2008. The National Transportation Safety Board also reiterates recommendations to the Federal Railroad Administration and the Association of American Railroads and reclassifies three recommendations to the Federal Railroad Administration.

Contents

Figures

Tables

Abbreviations and Acronyms

AAR	Association of American Railroads
AME	aviation medical examiner
Amtrak	National Railroad Passenger Corporation
BLET	Brotherhood of Locomotive Engineers and Trainmen
BMI	body mass index
BNSF	BNSF Railway
CFR	*Code of Federal Regulations*
CN	Canadian National Railroad
CRM	crew resource management
CSX	CSX Transportation
FAA	Federal Aviation Administration
FCC	Federal Communications Commission
FIRE	functionally integrated railroad equipment
FMCSA	Federal Motor Carrier Safety Administration
FRA	Federal Railroad Administration
KCSR	Kansas City Southern Railway Company
LOSA	Line Operations Safety Audit
MP	milepost
nm	nanometers
Norfolk Southern	Norfolk Southern Corporation
NTSB	National Transportation Safety Board
PTC	positive train control
RSAC	Railroad Safety Advisory Committee
RSIA	Rail Safety Improvement Act of 2008
UP	Union Pacific Railroad
SMS	safety management system
UTU	United Transportation Union

Executive Summary

On Sunday, June 24, 2012, at 10:02 a.m. central daylight time, eastbound Union Pacific Railroad (UP) freight train ZLAAH-22 and westbound UP freight train AAMMLX-22 collided head-on while operating on straight track on the UP Pratt subdivision near Goodwell, Oklahoma. Skies were clear, the temperature was 89°F, and visibility was 10 miles.

The collision derailed 3 locomotives and 24 cars of the eastbound train and 2 locomotives and 8 cars of the westbound train. The engineer and the conductor of the eastbound train and the engineer of the westbound train were killed. The conductor of the westbound train jumped to safety. During the collision and derailment, several fuel tanks from the derailed locomotives ruptured, releasing diesel fuel that ignited and burned. Damage was estimated at $14.8 million.

The National Transportation Safety Board determines that the probable cause of this accident was the eastbound Union Pacific Railroad train crew's lack of response to wayside signals because of the engineer's inability to see and correctly interpret the signals; the conductor's disengagement from his duties; and the lack of positive train control, which would have stopped the train and prevented the collision regardless of the crew's inaction. Contributing to the accident was a medical examination process that failed to decertify the engineer before his deteriorating vision adversely affected his ability to operate a train safely.

The accident investigation focused on the following safety issues:

- **The actions and responsibilities of the train crews:** Crew conversations in the locomotive cab concerning signal aspects, radio transmissions, or any condition that can affect the safe operation of the train are important crew activities. In this accident, as the train passed signals for advance approach, approach, and stop, the engineer actively adjusted the throttle and dynamic brake as if all three signals were clear. The fact that the conductor was disengaged from his duties and did not appropriately intervene as the train proceeded through the signals demonstrates a serious failure of the UP's safety management system that allowed lagging implementation of crew resource management.

- **The medical examination process for railroad engineer certification:** The UP's medical records for the engineer of the eastbound train indicated that the engineer had passed his required vision test in 2009. However, the medical records from the engineer's personal physician, his ophthalmologist, and his optometrist documented that his vision could not be corrected with glasses and contact lenses to meet the Federal Railroad Administration's (FRA) visual acuity requirements. In 2009, for the first time, the engineer also failed the color vision test accepted by the FRA. Although he passed the UP's color vision field test for secondary testing, the validity and reliability of that test are unknown. Although the FRA regulations allow such secondary tests, they do not define the characteristics of such tests to assure they are valid and reliable. Finally, no attempt was made to increase the frequency of medical evaluation when the railroad was aware that the engineer's vision was deteriorating from a chronic, progressive condition.

- **The survivability of event recorder data:** The lead and trailing locomotives of both trains in this accident had event recorders to capture and preserve operational data that is important to accident investigation. However, most of the data could not be retrieved after the severe damage to the lead locomotives from the postaccident fire. What data were retrieved were downloaded from a trailing locomotive, but the amount of data relayed to the trailing locomotive was much less than the data captured by the recorders on the front of the train. And even though the event recorders on the lead locomotives had certified crashworthy memory modules, they did not survive the fire. If more of the locomotive operating data had been relayed to the recorder on the trailing locomotive or to another location, information critical to the investigation of the accident would likely have survived the accident.

- **The need for implementation of positive train control:** Before reaching the Goodwell siding, the eastbound train crew had passed three signals without appropriately responding by slowing and then stopping their train. Regardless of the reason for the crew's nonresponse, had a positive train control system been in place in the area of the accident, it would have slowed and stopped the train, avoiding the collision.

As a result of this investigation, the National Transportation Safety Board makes safety recommendations to the Federal Railroad Administration, the Brotherhood of Locomotive Engineers and Trainmen, the United Transportation Union, all Class I Railroads, the Union Pacific Railroad, and all railroads subject to the positive train control provisions of the Rail Safety Improvement Act of 2008. The National Transportation Safety Board also reiterates recommendations to the Federal Railroad Administration and the Association of American Railroads and reclassifies three recommendations to the Federal Railroad Administration.

1 Investigation and Analysis

1.1 Accident Narrative

On Sunday, June 24, 2012, at 10:02 a.m. central daylight time,[1] eastbound Union Pacific Railroad (UP) freight train ZLAAH-22 (eastbound train) and westbound UP freight train AAMMLX-22 (westbound train) collided head-on while operating on straight track on the UP Pratt subdivision near Goodwell, Oklahoma. (See figure 1.) Skies were clear, the temperature was 89°F, and visibility was 10 miles.

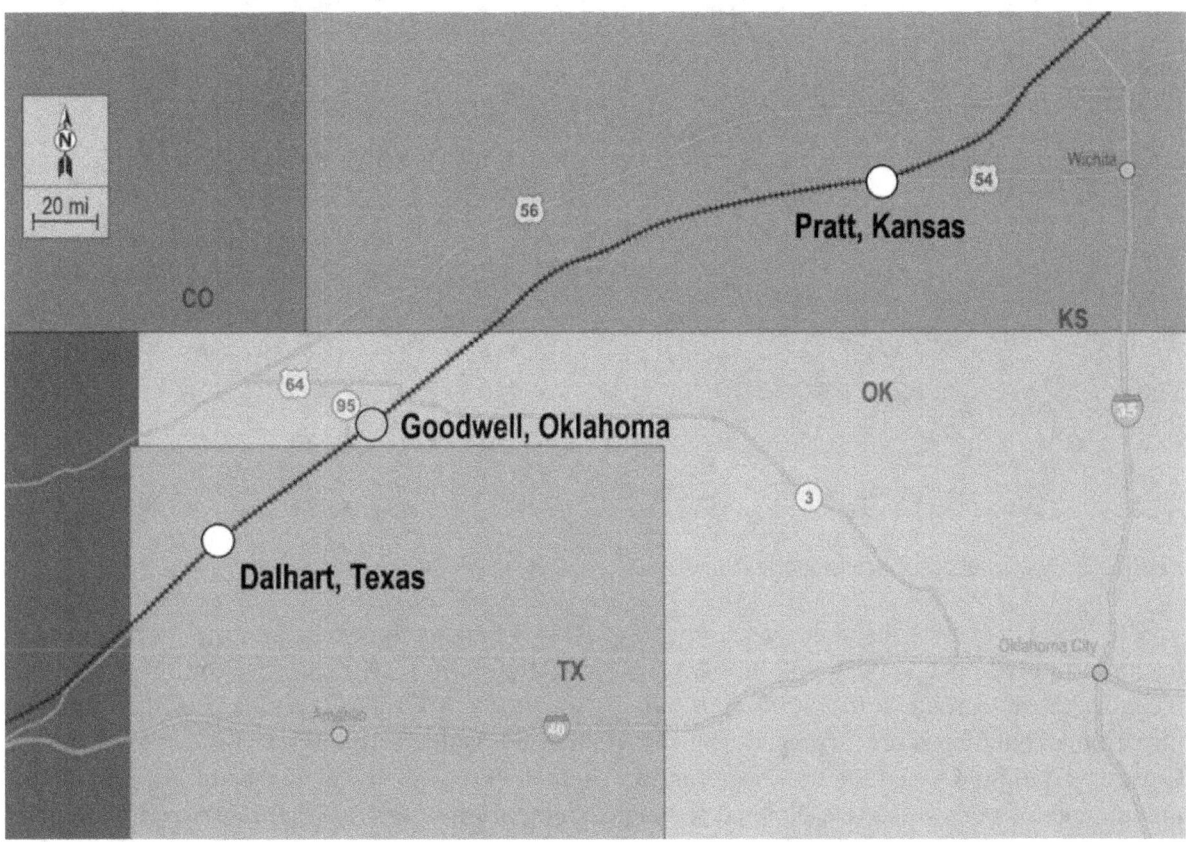

Figure 1. Map showing route of both trains on June 24, 2012, with collision location at Goodwell, Oklahoma.

The collision derailed 3 locomotives and 24 cars of the eastbound train and 2 locomotives and 8 cars of the westbound train. The engineer and the conductor of the eastbound train and the engineer of the westbound train were killed. The westbound train conductor jumped to safety. During the collision and derailment, several locomotive fuel tanks ruptured, releasing diesel fuel that ignited and burned. (See figure 2.) Damage was estimated at $14.8 million.

---

[1] All times in this report are central daylight time.

Figure 2. Aerial view of accident and fire.

The UP train dispatcher was controlling 10 to 12 trains in the area on the morning of the accident, including several trains operating both east and west over the division. This required the dispatcher to route some trains into sidings to meet other trains operating in the opposing direction. The dispatcher arranged for the eastbound and westbound trains to meet at the Goodwell siding by setting the combination of switches and signal lights to coordinate the movements of both trains. He planned for the eastbound train to stop on the main track, west of the east end of the Goodwell siding, and wait until the westbound train pulled into the siding and cleared the main track. The eastbound train would then continue east.[2]

In the territory of the accident, the UP signal system consisted of a clearly defined arrangement of colored lights (green, yellow, red) on the top of track-side masts to control the movement of trains in the east and west directions. Some signals had an additional lower light, to allow for additional signal indications (See figure 3.)

---

[2] According to dispatcher log data and the dispatcher's interview, the dispatcher had lined the switch for the westbound train to enter the siding, while the eastbound train was to stop at the stop signal at milepost 483.7.

Figure 3. Typical signal light on UP Pratt subdivision.

The westbound train originated in Kansas City, Kansas, with a final destination of Los Angeles, California. The train crew boarded in Pratt, Kansas, about 188 miles from Goodwell, and departed Pratt at 5:32 a.m. According to the conductor, the crew had an uneventful trip before they encountered an advance approach signal (flashing yellow light) at milepost (MP) 478.6, which required the train crew to reduce the train speed to 40 mph and be prepared to stop at the second signal. According to event recorder data and calculation of the motion at the front of the train, the train crew reduced speed to comply with the signal indication. The lead locomotive was moving at 51 mph when it passed MP 478.6, and it decelerated to 41 mph about 2 minutes later. At MP 481.2, the crew encountered an approach diverging signal indication (yellow-over-yellow light). Near MP 482.0, the crew saw the headlight of the eastbound train. After several seconds, the crew determined that the eastbound train had not stopped before it reached the east end of the Goodwell siding, as expected. The conductor and the engineer both placed the train air brakes into an emergency application. The conductor exited the locomotive cab and jumped to safety.

The eastbound train originated in Los Angeles, California, with a final destination of Chicago, Illinois. The train crew boarded at Dalhart, Texas, about 59 miles west of Goodwell, and departed at 8:45 a.m. The crew did not report anything unusual after leaving Dalhart. The track speed limit in the area where the accident occurred was 70 mph. Event recorder data showed that the train was operating at about 65 mph as it approached the accident location. At MP 487.9, the train encountered an advance approach signal (flashing yellow light), which required the train crew to reduce the train speed to 40 mph. Event recorder data showed that the engineer did not decrease train speed after the train passed the advance approach signal. About 2 miles beyond the advance approach signal, the eastbound train crew encountered an approach signal (solid yellow light over solid red light) at MP 485.5 (at the west end of the Goodwell siding). This signal required the train crew to reduce the train speed to 30 mph and be prepared to stop before passing the next signal. Event recorder data showed that the train crew did not reduce speed after the train passed the approach signal. About 2 miles beyond the approach signal, at MP 483.7 (the east end of the Goodwell siding), the eastbound train crew encountered a stop signal (solid red light) at which they were supposed to come to a stop. Event recorder data showed that the engineer did not stop for this signal; instead, the train passed the stop signal at about 65 mph. Immediately after passing the stop signal, the train went through a switch that had been aligned so that the westbound train would enter the Goodwell siding.[3] Event recorder data showed that the eastbound train's air brakes were placed into an emergency application about 8 seconds before impact with the westbound train. The two trains collided at MP 482.18.

While observing the train movements on the computer screen, the train dispatcher noticed the track circuit indication for the switch at the east end of the Goodwell siding start to flash, indicating that a switch was out of correspondence.[4] The train dispatcher immediately made several attempts to contact both train crews by radio but was unable to do so. He then checked with another train crew in the area to confirm that his radio was working properly. A short time later, the conductor of the westbound train used his cell phone to report the accident to the dispatcher.

At the time of impact, the eastbound train was traveling at 58 mph, and the westbound train was traveling at 21 mph. The lead locomotives of both trains were found on their sides, with extensive damage, in the field adjacent to the point of collision. Based on the locomotive event recorders on the trailing locomotives of each train and signal and dispatcher recorder data, the time of the collision was 10:02 a.m. Figure 4 shows a track map of the accident area.

---

[3] NTSB investigators examined the switch points at MP 483.7 and saw fresh contact marks on the field side, a gap between each switch and its stock rail, and a severely bent rod that controlled the position of the switch. These marks and conditions are consistent with the appearance of a switch that has been run through in the wrong direction.

[4] *Out of correspondence* refers to a condition in which a track switch is not lined and not locked.

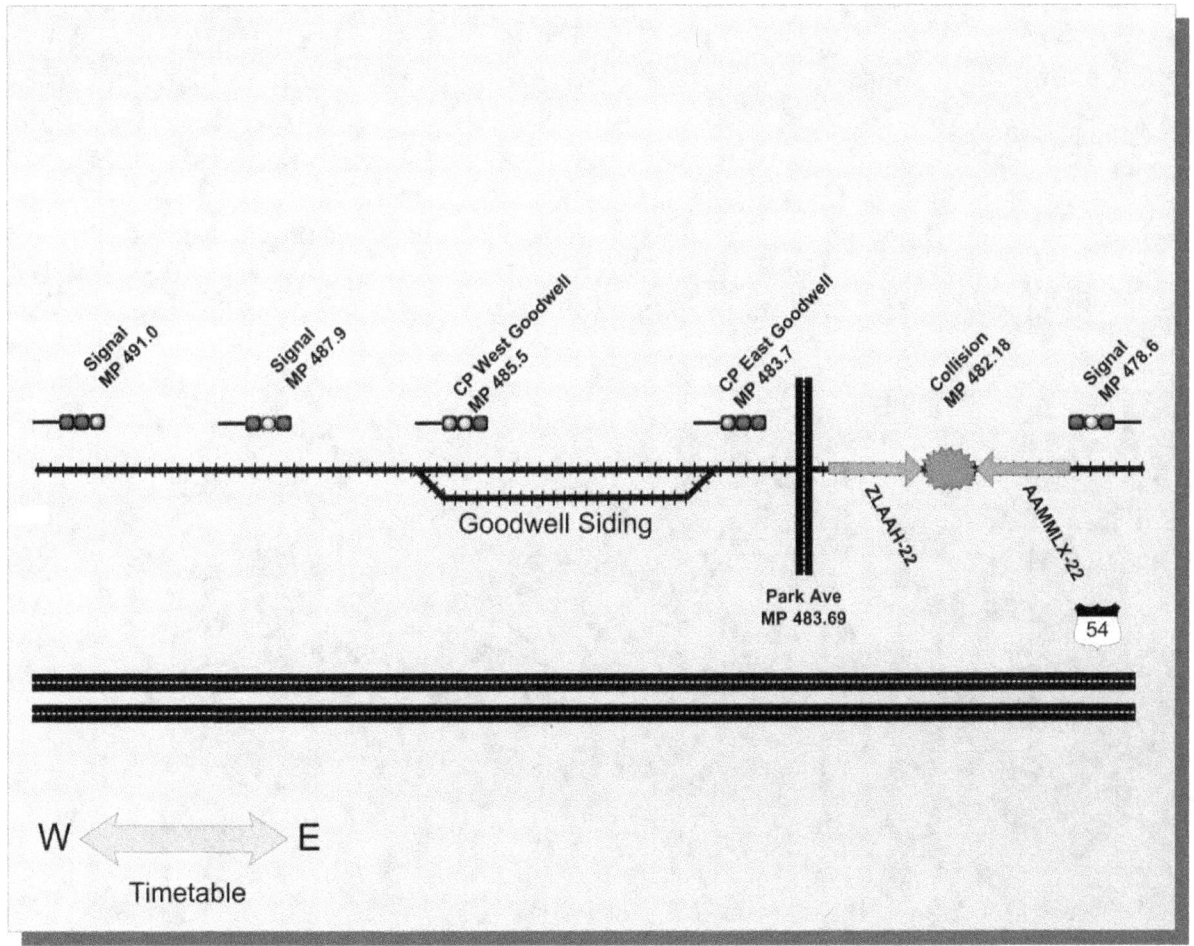

Figure 4. Track map of accident area.

The conductor of the westbound train told National Transportation Safety Board (NTSB) investigators that the trip had been normal until after the train passed Guymon, Oklahoma. He recalled passing an advance approach signal and said he knew the train would be entering a siding. When the conductor looked out of the window, he saw the headlight of the eastbound train. The conductor recalled the engineer's slowing the train and asking if the oncoming train looked close, to which the conductor replied that it was still coming. He said he then realized that the train was approaching much faster than he had initially thought. The conductor said he then told the engineer they had to jump; he last saw the engineer standing at the control stand. The conductor said he moved to the exit at the front of the train and saw smoke coming from the wheels of the oncoming train, which did not appear to be slowing down. At that point, he jumped from the train and saw a large explosion as he jumped.

The derailed locomotives and railcars of both trains came to rest as a pile of wreckage and debris near the point of collision. Witnesses told investigators that the wreckage was immediately engulfed in a large fire. The diesel-fueled fire burned for more than 24 hours despite fire suppression efforts that continued throughout the day and into the evening. (See figure 5.)

Figure 5. Suppression of the fire.

1.2 Factors Not Contributing to the Accident

On the morning of the accident, the weather was dry and no ground level visibility problems were reported. After the accident, the track, the signal system, the trailing locomotives, and the railcars were examined and tested by NTSB investigators. No defects were identified. Further, both trains had received initial terminal airbrake inspections before the accident, and no discrepancies were noted. Signal system data indicated that the signals were functioning properly up to and at the time of the collision. Investigators performed sight distance tests that simulated the movement of the eastbound train at same time and with the same weather conditions as on the day of the accident. All three signals that the eastbound train passed before reaching the east end of the Goodwell siding were clearly visible to a person with normal vision.

The surviving crewmember—the conductor of the westbound train—was tested in accordance with regulations; he did not have alcohol or drugs in his system. Investigators obtained usage records from known cell phone numbers for all four crewmembers; there was no cell phone activity for any of the crewmembers just before or at the time of the collision. The NTSB concludes that the following were not factors in the accident: the weather; the condition of the track, the locomotives, or the railcars; the signal system; cell phone use by any of the crewmembers; or drug or alcohol use by the conductor of the westbound train.

1.3 Limitations of the Investigation

This investigation was limited by the destruction by fire of the lead locomotives and their contents. The intensity of the postaccident fire precluded conducting autopsies or toxicology analyses of any of the deceased crewmembers. No personal effects of the crewmembers were recovered. The lead locomotives of both trains had functionally integrated railroad equipment (FIRE) computers that sent operating data to certified crashworthy event recorder memory modules. However, the long and intense postaccident fire destroyed both computers, and although the memory modules were recovered, they were so severely damaged that no data could be recovered.

1.4 Personnel Information

The engineer of the eastbound train was 56 years old. He was hired by the UP on July 28, 1995. UP records indicated that he passed his most recent physical examination, which included vision and hearing tests, to operate as an engineer on August 12, 2009. He was recertified to operate as a locomotive engineer on September 23, 2009; the recertification was valid until September 14, 2012. UP records also indicated that the engineer had taken and passed 96 railroad training courses between August 29, 1995, and May 31, 2012. The courses covered various aspects of railroad operations, and some courses included management oversight to ensure employees' knowledge and application of, and compliance with, railroad rules, regulations, and instructions. UP records from the year before the accident contained no disciplinary actions pertaining to the engineer.

The conductor of the eastbound train was 49 years old. He began work at the UP on May 19, 2003. According to UP records, the conductor had passed his most recent physical examination on January 18, 2008. UP records also indicated that the conductor had taken and passed 72 training courses between May 20, 2003 and January 17, 2012. UP records from the year before the accident contained no disciplinary actions pertaining to the conductor.

The engineer of the westbound train was 49 years old. He was hired by the UP on July 10, 1995. UP records indicated that the engineer had passed his most recent physical examination, which included vision and hearing tests, on December 9, 2009. He was recertified to operate as a locomotive engineer on February 10, 2010; the recertification was valid until March 7, 2013. UP records further indicated that the engineer had taken and passed 94 training courses between October 22, 1996, and May 3, 2012. The training courses covered various aspects of railroad operations, and some courses included management oversight to ensure employees' knowledge and application of, and compliance with, railroad rules, regulations, and instructions. UP records from the year before the accident contained no disciplinary actions pertaining to the engineer.

The conductor of the westbound train was 34 years old. He began work at the UP on May 19, 2003. UP records indicated that the conductor had passed his most recent physical examination on February 20, 2009. UP records also indicated that the conductor had taken and passed 70 training courses between May 19, 2003, and December 24, 2011. UP records from the year before the accident contained no disciplinary actions pertaining to the conductor.

The crewmembers of both UP trains were trained and tested, and they were qualified by the UP to perform their duties.

1.4.1 Job Responsibilities of Engineer and Conductor

Crewmembers who operate trains on the UP have clear responsibilities. These responsibilities are documented in the UP operating rulebook, which is based on the sixth edition of the *General Code of Operating Rules* (GCOR),[5] effective April 7, 2010. Specifically, the conductor is in charge of the train and must remind the locomotive engineer of any upcoming restrictions. The engineer is responsible for safely and efficiently operating the engine. Crewmembers must obey instructions from the locomotive engineer that concern operating the engine. Crew conversations in the locomotive cab concerning signal aspects and radio transmissions are an important crew activity. UP management makes in-cab signal aspect conversations among crewmembers an important part of its crew-monitoring program.

The UP operating rulebook (UP 2010) states the following crewmember responsibilities:

C. All Crewmembers' Responsibilities

1. To ensure the train is operated safely and rules are observed, all crewmembers must act responsibly to prevent accidents or rule violations. Crewmembers in the engine control compartment must communicate to each other any restrictions or other known conditions that affect the safe operation of their train sufficiently in advance of such condition to allow the engineer to take proper action. If proper action is not being taken, crewmembers must remind engineer of such condition and required action.

2. Crewmembers in the engine control compartment must be alert for signals. As soon as signals become visible or audible, crewmembers must communicate clearly to each other the name of signals affecting their train. They must continue to observe signals and announce any change of aspect until the train passes the signal. If the signal is not complied with promptly, crewmembers must remind the engineer and/or conductor of the rule requirement. If crewmembers do not agree on the signal indication, regard the signal as the most restrictive indication observed.

---

[5] The GCOR is a standard book of operating rules adopted by many railroads in the United States. It was developed by a committee composed of adopting railroads and is updated periodically by the committee. Each railroad that adopts the GCOR remains free to modify the specific rules to better suit its individual operating characteristics.

3. When the engineer and/or conductor fail to comply with a signal indication or take proper action to comply with a restriction or rule, crewmembers must immediately take action to ensure safety, using the emergency brake valve to stop the train, if necessary. (UP 2010, 1-29)

Both the conductor and the locomotive engineer must announce to each other in the locomotive cab the aspect of all signals encountered. If any signal is displaying an aspect that is less than clear,[6] the crew must also announce the train identification and the aspect in a radio transmission to the dispatcher and trains in the area. There are no radio recordings, nor were they required, from the accident at Goodwell, Oklahoma, therefore it cannot be determined whether any signals were announced on the radio.

1.4.2 Eastbound Train Crew Performance

Evidence of the actions of the eastbound train was obtained from the event recorder on the trailing locomotive and the wayside signal logs. The advance approach signal (flashing yellow light) was about 2 miles from the approach signal and about 4 miles from the stop signal at the east end of the Goodwell siding. The advance approach signal required the crew to slow their train to 40 mph. The approach signal (solid yellow light over solid red light) required the crew to proceed at not more than 30 mph and be prepared to stop at the next signal (red light), which was a stop signal. The stop signal required the crew to stop the train. The crew did not comply with any of the three wayside signals; instead, the train was operated past each of the signals at speeds greater than 60 mph, ultimately colliding head-on with the westbound train. (See figure 6.) The investigation revealed that the advance approach, approach, and stop signals were functioning properly and accurately displayed their aspects before the accident.

---

[6] A *clear* (green) signal indication allows a train to operate at the maximum speed authorized for the track segment. A less-than-clear signal is one that is more restrictive than a clear (green) signal indication.

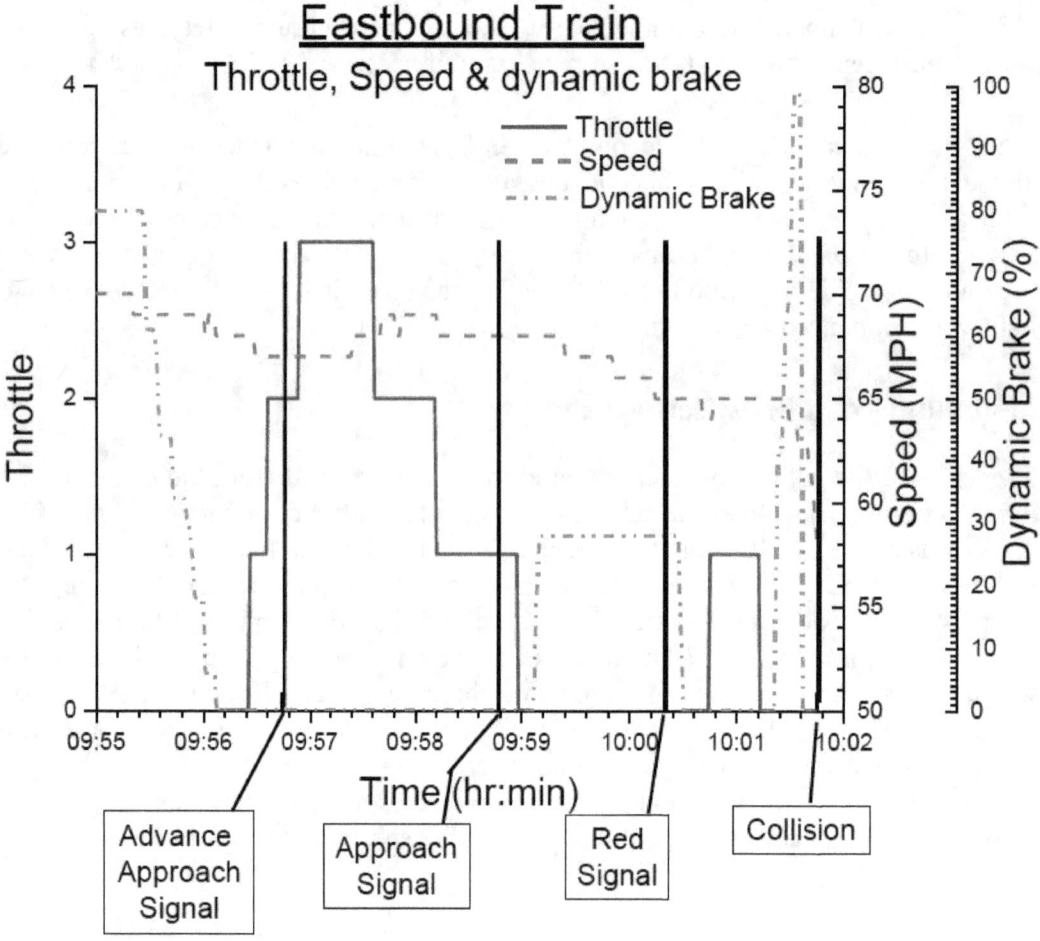

Figure 6. Eastbound train timeline using event recorder data from trailing locomotive.

The eastbound train engineer did not reduce the train speed in accordance with the two approach signals or stop the train at the third (last) signal—a stop signal—before the collision. Instead, based on the event recorder data, the engineer appeared to make throttle and dynamic brake adjustments that maintained train speed close to the 70 mph limit, as would be expected for a train operating on a clear signal. The conductor did not intervene to slow or stop the train as the wayside signals were not obeyed, as required by UP rules. At the time of the accident, the conductor of the eastbound train had worked for the UP for 9 years. Given his years of experience, it seems unlikely that he saw the advance approach, approach, and stop signals and chose to do nothing to stop the train in time to prevent the collision. It seems much more likely that the conductor failed to observe the three signals during the almost 5 minutes between the advance approach signal and the collision. It appears that he was not engaged in the developing situation as the train neared and proceeded past the advance approach signal. However, detailed evidence that would have been useful to reconstruct and explain the circumstances leading to the accident was limited due to the extensive collision damage and fire: there were no data on crew behavior captured in the event recorder on the lead locomotive, no autopsy results, no toxicology information, and no data from the conductor's personal electronic devices, and his personal possessions on board the train did not survive. The NTSB therefore concludes that for undetermined reasons the conductor of the eastbound train was disengaged from performing his duties as the train passed the advance approach, approach, and stop signals.

Despite the lack of available evidence, the investigation considered plausible scenarios based on available evidence and experience with past railroad accidents to explain the erroneous operation of the eastbound train. The investigation looked for indications that the crewmembers may have been unable or otherwise prevented from operating the train. The trailing unit event recorder data indicated that throttle and dynamic brake adjustments were made in the minutes prior to the collision. Moreover, there was no indication of distress from the train, either by radio calls or by emergency braking until seconds before the collision. Therefore, it is unlikely that a situation existed in the locomotive cab that prevented both crewmembers from making train control actions.

The investigation also considered scenarios in which the crew became disoriented or confused about their track location. Notwithstanding the crew's noncompliance with three wayside signals, a witness to the accident, who was driving a truck parallel to the eastbound train for several miles, reported to investigators that the train horn was blown at a highway crossing a few miles before the accident. Thus, it seems unlikely that the crewmembers were disoriented or confused about their location.

The available evidence for the actions of the eastbound train crew does suggest that the crewmembers performed in a disengaged, if not dysfunctional, manner. Specifically, an operating practice across the railroad industry is that both crewmembers are responsible for the overall safe and efficient movement of the train. Moreover, it is known that effective crew coordination is imperative for safe operations involving two or more crewmembers. Since both crewmembers were present in the locomotive cab (based on recovery evidence), and since both crewmembers failed to comply with the wayside signals, the NTSB concludes that both crewmembers of the eastbound train failed to maintain proper crew coordination and jointly failed to make proper decisions and actions to control the train safely.

Many accidents in transportation systems occur because of poor decisions and actions by people, as opposed to machinery failures. Consequently, approaches to minimize and avoid these human factors failures have received considerable attention over the past 2 decades across several transportation industries: aviation, maritime, pipeline, and railroad transportation. One of the more successful approaches is crew resource management (CRM), which makes use of equipment, procedures, and people to achieve greater levels of safety and efficiency in system operations.

The main principle of CRM is that crewmembers will work together safely when their work climate fosters effective communications, improved situation awareness, and good leadership. Safety studies have indicated that CRM increases crew work relationships, improves control of workload levels, enhances exchange of mission information, increases cross-monitoring performance, improves management of mission-threatening errors, and increases the number of successful mission segments. In the aviation industry, the organizational impact of CRM has been a decrease in the number of aircraft accidents.

The purpose of CRM is to assure that all crewmembers understand their roles and responsibilities in relation to the tasks being performed. Teamwork and active engagement are important elements of CRM. Moreover, CRM becomes even more important when one or more members of a crew potentially become disengaged, distracted, or performs in a dysfunctional manner, and, therefore, the whole system is at higher risk of failure. Using CRM principles of effective communications, situation awareness, and teamwork can mitigate the adverse risks of poor individual and team performance.

The NTSB has identified the lack of CRM as a safety failure in previous railroad accidents. In its investigation of a March 25, 1998, collision between two Norfolk Southern Corporation (Norfolk Southern) trains in Butler, Indiana, the NTSB concluded that railroad safety would be improved if crewmembers received CRM training (NTSB 1999). As a result of the Butler, Indiana, accident, the NTSB issued safety recommendations to the Federal Railroad Administration (FRA), Norfolk Southern, Class I railroads and Amtrak (National Railroad Passenger Corporation), the American Short Line and Regional Railroad Association, the Brotherhood of Locomotive Engineers, and the United Transportation Union (UTU) to work together to develop and implement CRM training for train crewmembers.

Likewise, NTSB investigated the September 30, 2010, collision of two Canadian National Railway freight trains near Two Harbors, Minnesota (NTSB 2013b). The trains were operating in unsignaled territory, and one train entered the main track from a siding after failing to properly execute an after-arrival track authority.[7] All five crewmembers on the two trains were injured, and estimated damages were $8.1 million. The NTSB determined that inadequate CRM, as evidenced by disengaged and dysfunctional crew performance that allowed a lack of communications, unchallenged decisions, and rule violations, contributed to the probable cause of the accident.

In August 2012, NTSB investigators met with the FRA, which provided information on current efforts to facilitate the development and implementation of CRM in the rail industry. FRA representatives told the NTSB that the FRA was monitoring progress regarding CRM with select railroads. They also reported that FRA-sponsored research published since 2007 had led to CRM training curricula for transportation, mechanical, and engineering employees and had provided business-case justifications for CRM in the rail industry. Moreover, FRA had awarded grants to some railroads, including the UP, for CRM pilot programs. Therefore, the NTSB concludes that there is an adequate foundation of guidance and opportunity for railroads to develop and deploy CRM programs.

At the February 26, 2013, investigative hearing on the Goodwell accident held at NTSB headquarters (NTSB 2013c), the UP testified that it uses CRM and other crew safety programs, such as peer-to-peer oversight and confidential close-call reporting, within its railroad system, but it had not implemented these programs yet on the Pratt subdivision where the Goodwell collision occurred. The NTSB concludes that had crewmembers of the eastbound train received training in and practiced the principles of CRM and other crew safety programs, they likely

---

[7] With an *after-arrival track authority*, the permission to occupy a designated portion of single main track does not become effective until after the arrival of one or more opposing trains.

would have demonstrated improved coordination, communication, and discipline while operating the train.

One crew safety program discussed by the UP during the hearing involved peer-to-peer oversight. Experience in other transportation modes indicates that the use of peer observers in a nonpunitive program to assess operational safety, perform peer-to-peer counseling, and generate data on trends of risky behaviors that can be used to develop mitigation strategies is an approach with merit. For example, the aviation industry has found success in the Line Operations Safety Audit (LOSA), a voluntary safety program in which trained observers (usually line pilots from the airline) ride on a jump seat during regularly scheduled flights to collect safety-related data on environmental conditions, operational complexity, training efficacy, and flight crew performance. The data collected remain confidential, and pilots are assured of nonpunitive use of those data.

The LOSA program is a proactive means to understand the flight management process—both successful and unsuccessful—by noting the problems crews encounter on the line and how they manage these problems. Such a program would be equally valuable to the rail industry, as suggested by the circumstances of the Two Harbors, Minnesota, accident. The NTSB is aware that a few railroads have begun the implementation of LOSA-like programs. The NTSB concludes that a nonpunitive peer audit program is an important element of an effective safety management system (SMS) and would provide railroads with opportunities to better understand and address operational safety issues. Therefore, the NTSB recommends that the UP work with the Brotherhood of Locomotive Engineers and Trainmen (BLET) and the UTU to develop and implement a nonpunitive peer audit program focused on rule compliance and operational safety. Also, the NTSB recommends that the BLET work with the UP and the UTU to develop and implement a nonpunitive peer audit program focused on rule compliance and operational safety for the UP. Further, the NTSB recommends that the UTU work with the UP and the BLET to develop and implement a nonpunitive peer audit program focused on rule compliance and operational safety for the UP. It is important to note that CRM and LOSA are components of an overall SMS; that is, they are facets of a systematic approach to manage safety risks throughout all levels of an organization. SMS provides for goal setting, planning, and measuring safety performance, including the following:

- How an organization is set up to manage risk

- Identification of workplace risks and suitable controls

- Implementation of effective communications across all levels of an organization

- Implementation of processes to identify and correct nonconformities

- Implementation of continual improvement processes

In other words, an effective SMS requires organizational structures, accountabilities, policies, and procedures that ensure diligent and aggressive implementation of management's safety objectives throughout the workforce. All federally regulated transportation industries have recognized the importance of SMS as a foundation for a robust safety culture. It is known that an effective SMS helps companies reduce and prevent accidents and reduce accident-related loss of life, time, and resources, including money.

The Goodwell investigation revealed a failure in the UP SMS. Despite the UP's acknowledgment of the importance of SMS and its intent to implement crew safety programs throughout its railroad system, the UP admits that it has not achieved this safety goal yet, and, in particular, it has not implemented CRM and related crew safety programs on the Pratt subdivision. The UP testified that more time is needed to implement the program, despite its recognition that a SMS allows it to identify, mitigate, and manage safety risks to its workforce and the public. The NTSB is concerned that the UP continues to operate its trains, especially in the Pratt subdivision, without a fully implemented and mature SMS. Therefore, the NTSB concludes that had the UP established, maintained, and enforced a SMS, it is likely that this accident may have been avoided. The NTSB recommends that the UP develop and implement a plan to establish a SMS, which incorporates CRM.

1.4.3 Fatigue

The NTSB routinely examines the potential role of human fatigue in accident scenarios. Human fatigue is known to arise from lifestyle routines that limit or create variations in sleep patterns, medical conditions and medications that create drowsiness, as well as an array of physiological and psychological stress factors that create weary reactions to operational requirements. Consequentially, the NTSB works to determine the likelihood of human fatigue and its significance in accident causation by carefully considering numerous human factors.

In the Goodwell accident investigation, many of the information sources used to assess human fatigue factors were destroyed by the casualties and the fire resulting from the train collision, as well as by the associated emergency response recovery work. Nevertheless, the information obtained on the likelihood of fatigue for the eastbound crewmembers—primarily from UP work records and interviews with surviving family members—is discussed below.

Table 1 shows the work schedule for the eastbound engineer for 4 days leading up to the accident. On the day of the accident, the engineer reported for duty at 6:40 a.m., and the accident occurred 3 hours 21 minutes later. The day before the accident, the engineer was off duty. He lived with his mother, who was unable to discuss her son's non-work activities and sleep patterns with investigators. However, it was determined from UP work records that during the second and third days before the accident, the engineer had worked nights, starting about 10:00 p.m. and finishing at irregular morning hours. His work schedule indicates that he had an irregular schedule, and, consequentially, irregular opportunities to sleep, which is a known factor causing human fatigue. However, event recorder data for the eastbound train indicated that before the collision, the engineer was making throttle and dynamic brake adjustments, indicating that he was not asleep. But, because a complete history of his non-work activities and his actual sleep patterns were not available to the investigation, the NTSB could not determine whether fatigue affected the engineer's operation of the train.

Table 1. Work schedule for engineer of eastbound train for 4 days before accident.

DATE	ON-DUTY	OFF-DUTY	WORK HOURS	NON-WORK HOURS	SLEEP OPPORTUNITY HOURS
Wednesday, June 20, 2012	10:15 p.m.				
		9:45 a.m.	12.50		
Thursday, June 21, 2012				12.25	up to 12.25
	10:00 p.m.				
Friday, June 22, 2012		2:45 a.m.	5.75		
Saturday, June 23, 2012				24.00	up to 24.00
Sunday, June 24, 2012	6:40 a.m.				
		10:01 a.m.	3.35		

Table 2 shows the work schedule for the conductor of the eastbound train for 4 days leading up to the accident. On the day of the accident, he reported for work at 6:40 a.m.; the eastbound engineer reported for work at the same time. The conductor's spouse reported that he went to bed about 10:00 p.m. on June 23, suggesting that he had no more than about 8 hours of sleep opportunity before work on the day of the accident. For the 2 days before the accident, the conductor was off duty, but his non-work activities and his sleep patterns were not available to the investigation. And for 2 days before this 2-day off-duty period, the conductor reported for work at varying night and day times, although no further information about his non-work periods and sleep patterns was available to the investigation. The conductor's work schedule indicates that he also had an irregular work schedule, and, therefore, irregular opportunities to sleep. But because the non-work activities and actual sleep patterns of the conductor were unavailable to the investigation, the NTSB could not determine whether fatigue affected the conductor's operation of the train.

Table 2. Work schedule for conductor of eastbound train for 4 days before accident.

DATE	ON-DUTY	OFF-DUTY	WORK HOURS	NON-WORK HOURS	SLEEP OPPORTUNITY HOURS
Wednesday, June 20, 2012	1:05 a.m.				
		1:00 p.m.	12.08		
				12.25	up to 12.25
Thursday, June 21, 2012	9:30 a.m.				
		1:05 p.m.	3.58		
Friday, June 22, 2012				24.00	up to 24.00
Saturday, June 23, 2012				24.00	up to 8.00
Sunday, June 24, 2012	6:40 a.m.				
		10:01 a.m.	3.35		

The UP work records indicated that in the week before the accident, both crewmembers of the eastbound train had been called to work at various times of the day and night. However, the circumstances of the accident resulted in a substantial loss of evidence and traceability of the actions and reactions of the engineer and the conductor before the collision. Therefore, the NTSB concludes that insufficient information was available to determine whether fatigue of the eastbound train crew was a factor in the accident.

1.4.4 Train Crew Medical Requirements

Federal regulations require railroad personnel in safety-sensitive positions[8] to undergo a medical evaluation that is limited to measuring vision and hearing. The regulations have no requirements for evaluating any other health concerns or medication use. Engineers have been subject to this requirement for almost 22 years. Conductors were added with nearly identical requirements, in Title 49 *Code of Federal Regulations* (CFR) 242.117, effective September 1, 2012.

Title 49 CFR 240.121 requires railroad engineers to meet the following vision criteria, and 49 CFR 240.201 requires railroad engineers to meet these criteria every 3 years:

(1) For distant viewing either:

(i) Distant visual acuity of at least 20/40 (Snellen)[9] in each eye without corrective lenses or

(ii) Distant visual acuity separately corrected to at least 20/40 (Snellen) with corrective lenses and distant binocular acuity of at least 20/40 (Snellen) in both eyes with or without corrective lenses;

(2) A field of vision of at least 70 degrees in the horizontal meridian in each eye; and

(3) The ability to recognize and distinguish between the colors of railroad signals as demonstrated by successfully completing one of the tests in appendix F to [49 CFR 240.121].

1.4.5 Train Crew Medical Information

The UP provided the NTSB with its medical records for all crewmembers of both trains. According to those records, all four crewmembers had passed their most recent medical examinations and were certified at the time of the accident.

---

[8] A *safety-sensitive position* is one covered under the hours of service laws, including train and engine service employees involved in the movement of trains or engines (that is, engineers, conductors, brakemen, switchmen, locomotive hostlers/helpers); dispatching employees who issue mandatory directives (that is, train dispatchers, control operators); and signal employees who inspect, repair, or maintain signal systems.

[9] The *Snellen* chart measures visual acuity by comparing a person's ability to see relative to a person with normal vision. A person with 20/40 vision can accurately read information at a distance of 20 feet that a person with normal vision can accurately read at a distance of 40 feet.

The UP medical records for the westbound crewmembers documented no medical issues related to vision or hearing. The westbound engineer had a single measurement of height and weight on his preemployment exam in 1995. At that time, he was 72 inches tall, weighed 248.5 pounds, and reported treatment for hypertension on his new-hire physical in 1995. His body mass index (BMI)[10] was 33.6 (NHBLI 2013). The westbound conductor had a single measurement of his height and weight on his preemployment physical in 2003. At that time he was 67 inches tall and weighed 217 pounds (BMI = 34.0).

The eastbound train conductor's UP medical records did not identify any medical issues. He had passed all of his medical certification exams and did not report any medical problems to the railroad. On his preemployment physical in 2003, he was 71 inches tall and weighed 187 pounds (BMI = 26.1). However, during an interview with the NTSB, his wife reported a history of gout and treatment for mild hypertension.

The eastbound train engineer's UP medical records identified a number of medical conditions. On his preemployment exam in 1995 he was 73 inches tall and weighed 246 pounds (BMI = 32.5). He had entries related to a retinal detachment requiring months off the job in 2001–2002 and for injuries related to a motorcycle crash requiring weeks off the job in 2003. He had passed previous vision testing but initially failed both visual acuity and color vision testing in 2009. The follow-up evaluation of his vision in 2009 and his ongoing vision problems are discussed more extensively in the remainder of this section.

The NTSB obtained and reviewed additional personal medical records for the engineer of the eastbound train from three physicians and an optometrist.[11] The records from his primary care doctor show intermittent treatment for gout and occasional visits for upper respiratory infections, and the records demonstrate that his weight varied from about 245 to 259 pounds during the period from 2001 to 2012. In addition, for many years he had regular appointments with both an optometrist and an ophthalmologist.[12] In the year before the accident, the engineer regularly saw a second ophthalmologist who specialized in retinal care.

The engineer had multiple eye conditions that caused persistent vision problems and progressive vision loss. In childhood he had cataract surgery, which required removing the lenses from both of his eyes. This meant that he routinely required both contact lenses and glasses with progressive lenses to focus on distant, intermediate, and near objects. Of note, all of the visual acuity measurements included in this report were obtained with his contact lenses in and his glasses on.

In addition to having cataracts, the engineer had longstanding open-angle glaucoma[13] in both eyes. Glaucoma is a disorder in which the pressure inside the eye becomes and remains too

---

[10] BMI is a measure of body fat that applies to adults. Normal BMI is between 18.5 and 24.9, overweight is considered 25.0 to 29.9, and a BMI of more than 30.0 is considered obese.

[11] An *optometrist* is a vision specialist who may prescribe glasses and contact lenses.

[12] An *ophthalmologist* is a medical doctor who specializes in eye care and may prescribe medications and perform ocular surgical procedures.

[13] *Open-angle glaucoma* is a chronic eye disease associated with increased pressure in the eye that causes damage to the optic nerve. Glaucoma can degrade vision, leading to blindness.

high, putting pressure on the optic nerve and the retina. Untreated, it leads to blindness. To keep the pressures in his eyes in or close to the normal range, the engineer required daily medications. Over the years, when medications failed to sufficiently control the intraocular pressure, he required various procedures to decrease the pressure. The last of these procedures was the placement of a drain in his left eye in November 2009, which allowed fluid to come out to the edge of the sclera (the white outer layer of the eye) when the intraocular pressure became high. When needed, the fluid pocket is then drained by an ophthalmologist. The ophthalmologist performed this procedure on the engineer multiple times.

In his left eye, the engineer had recurrent episodes of iritis[14] and vitreitis[15] and had required a surgical procedure to remove and replace the vitreous in his left eye.[16] In his right eye, in addition to having previous cataract surgery and glaucoma, he had a retinal detachment requiring surgery in 2001. By 2011, as a result of all the inflammation from his eye diseases, he developed cystoid macular edema.[17] In addition, epiretinal membranes[18] caused wrinkling of the retina in both eyes. This required surgery to remove the membranes on his right eye in September 2011 and on his left eye in November 2011. These last two conditions cause wavy distorted areas in the central vision that appear something like looking through water droplets. The locations and extent of the visual distortion from these conditions may change significantly from day to day.

The engineer's medical records indicate that his vision was evaluated many times; some evaluations were required for his 3-year locomotive engineer recertification, as mandated in 49 CFR 240.121, while others were part of his ongoing medical care. His medical evaluations included tests of his near and distant visual acuity, peripheral field of view, and color discrimination. However, every 3 years from 1998 through 2006, the engineer passed the vision and hearing tests required by the FRA.

In 2006, his corrected vision was measured by his primary care physician for his railroad medical examination as 20/30 in both eyes for both near and distant visual acuity, he had a horizontal visual field of view of 90 degrees in each eye, and he passed the Ishihara color plate test without error (17 plates).[19]

Between 2006 and 2009, the engineer underwent a series of medical and surgical interventions for uncontrolled glaucoma, mostly in the left eye. According to his optometrist's and ophthalmologists' records, he had variable results on visual acuity testing; it was different on every visit. However, at no time after May 14, 2008, was the engineer's corrected vision in his left eye documented by any of his medical providers as better than 20/70. By 2009, he reported

---

[14] *Iritis* is a condition in which there is inflammation in the anterior chamber of the eye.

[15] *Vitreitis* is a condition in which there is inflammation in the posterior chamber of the eye.

[16] The *vitreous* is a gel-like substance that helps the eye maintain a round shape.

[17] *Cystoid macular edema* is swelling in the central area of the retina (the macula) caused by capillaries leaking fluid. It distorts central vision.

[18] An *epiretinal membrane* is created by local inflammation causing a thin film to develop over an area of the retina, usually in the macula. It can be a complication of cystoid macular edema, and it distorts vision.

[19] The Ishihara test is the standard protocol mentioned in 49 CFR Part 240, Appendix F, to test for color vision deficiencies.

to his medical providers that his visual acuity was sometimes "marginal" and quite variable and that he was having trouble with color vision.

On August 12, 2009, the engineer underwent testing at his primary care physician's office as part of his FRA-required triennial railroad medical examination. On that date, his corrected visual acuity did not meet the standard; it was measured as 20/80 in the right eye and 20/80 in the left eye. Also, he failed the Ishihara color plate testing, getting only 7 out of 17 plates correct. Only his peripheral vision met the standard. The visual acuity and color vision test failures should have disqualified him from recertification as a locomotive engineer, pending a retest or review by a railroad medical examiner.

The engineer sought assistance from his optometrist, likely hoping a new set of glasses would improve his visual acuity. During a visit on August 17, 2009, the optometrist attempted to correct the engineer's vision with glasses but was able to correct it to only 20/40-2 (meaning two errors at the 20/40 level) in the right eye and 20/70-2 in the left eye. There was no record of color vision testing by the optometrist. However, in the record from that visit, the optometrist quoted the engineer as saying he was "losing color recognition." The engineer provided the results from both his primary care doctor's testing and the optometrist's testing to the UP.

The synopsis of medical records provided by the UP to the NTSB included the following information:

> September 16, 2009—The [UP] chief medical officer reported speaking with [the optometrist], who said [the engineer] had a history of cataracts (and had lenses removed) and glaucoma. He said [the optometrist] reported that [the engineer's] current visual acuity was 20/40 in both eyes and full to confrontation.[20] He still needed color vision testing.

Based on the fact that no further visual acuity testing was required or performed, it appears that the UP used this conversation to determine that the engineer met the FRA requirements for visual acuity. The optometrist's records contained no record of this conversation or any record of visits by the engineer to the optometrist in 2009 after August 17. Nevertheless, the conversation recorded in the UP's records should have made it clear to the railroad that the deterioration in the engineer's vision was the result of glaucoma, a chronic and progressive disease. The NTSB concludes that the results from required medical examinations and UP conversations with the engineer's health care providers demonstrated to the UP that the eastbound train engineer's vision had significantly deteriorated because of a chronic medical condition.

After the UP medically certified the eastbound train engineer in 2009, the engineer's vision continued to deteriorate. He continued to require the procedure to relieve the intraocular pressure in his left eye, and his vision continued to fluctuate. In July 2010, he told his ophthalmologist that he had "noticed some trouble telling color on train traffic signals." In August 2010, he complained to his optometrist of "variable color vision." Also in August, the

---

[20] *Full to confrontation* is a normal result of confrontation testing for peripheral vision, but the test is designed to identify only significant defects. Confrontation testing is part of a physical examination aimed at determining the patient's peripheral vision by comparing it to the examiner's peripheral vision.

engineer's ophthalmologist administered the Farnsworth D-15 test, a color vision test that can determine the type and severity of color vision loss (Colblinder 2013). The engineer's results placed him in a category of severe protanopia, also known as red-blindness.[21] In people who have acquired severe protanopia, the red-detecting cones in the retina no longer function. This means that colors of light with wavelengths longer than about 490 nanometers (nm) appear as shades of yellow, and those with shorter wavelengths appear as shades of blue. Although the exact colors of railroad signal lights are not regulated, the Association of American Railroads (AAR) chromaticity standards for railroad signals place the red signals about 622 nm, yellow between 589 and 598 nm, and green between 498 and 512 nm. To the engineer, signals at these wavelengths would have appeared as various shades of yellow. Some people with color vision defects use differences in brightness to compensate for difficulty with color differences. However, in addition to having difficulty detecting color differences above 490 nm, people with protanopia perceive colors of longer wavelengths (green, yellow, orange, and red) as less bright than people with normal vision do.

Also in August 2010, the Texas Department of Motor Vehicles restricted the engineer's automobile driver's license to daytime driving only. A representative of the Texas Department of Motor Vehicles told the NTSB that there are only three reasons for such a restriction: at the request of the driver, when the driver verbally reported limited night vision, or when the result of visual acuity testing using both eyes was worse than 20/70. The representative was unable to tell the NTSB which of these was the reason for the engineer's license restriction, but because his visual acuity measured at the time by his eye-care providers ranged from 20/60 to 20/100 in both eyes, it seems likely that the restriction was placed as a result of deteriorating visual acuity.

Overall, between his last medical certification by the UP in September 2009 and the Goodwell accident in June 2012, the engineer visited his eye-care providers on more than 50 occasions and underwent 12 separate procedures. Some of these procedures were for elevated ocular pressure as a result of his glaucoma, but he also underwent two surgeries in 2011 to strip the epiretinal membranes from in front of his retinas. He continued to have cystoid macular edema, which causes variable areas of distortion within the central vision and can also impair color vision. He is quoted in 2011 as saying that his vision was "sometimes good and sometimes not" and noted "to have a hard time distinguishing colors." On his last visit, on June 4, 2012, his visual acuity was measured as 20/70 in the right eye and 20/200 in the left eye.

The engineer's vision continued to deteriorate following his last medical certification in 2009. Based on the engineer's years of professional experience and his corresponding knowledge of the signals in the subdivision in which he was operating, it is reasonable to expect he would have slowed and stopped the train had he seen and interpreted the wayside signals correctly. Instead, he operated the train as if the signal aspects were green. Based on the evidence of the operation of the train once it arrived at and proceeded beyond the advance approach, approach, and stop signals, the NTSB concludes that the engineer of the eastbound train was unable to visually detect and correctly interpret the wayside signals.

---

[21] *Protanopia* is a type of color vision defect in which only two hues are seen; colors appear bluish or yellowish because of a lack of perception of red and green. Colors with wavelengths below 493 nanometers appear bluish; colors with wavelengths above 493 nanometers (red and green) appear yellowish.

1.5 Adequacy of UP Medical Records

On September 16, 2009, the same day as the conversation between the optometrist and the UP chief medical officer, the engineer of the eastbound train saw his ophthalmologist. The ophthalmologist's records from that visit quote the engineer as stating that the optometrist "could only get to 20/70" in the left eye. On that day, the ophthalmologist measured the engineer's corrected vision as 20/70-2 in the right eye and 20/100-1 in the left eye. Based on the medical records made available to the NTSB, the engineer's visual acuity in his left eye was not measured as 20/40 or better by any clinician on or after September 16, 2009. The NTSB investigation did not find any written documentation of the engineer's visual acuity consistent with the reported conversation from the UP between the medical officer and the optometrist.

The UP's policy for verifying visual acuity was to obtain written documentation from an outside source stating the visual acuity test used and the crewmember's test results. The UP did not comply with this policy when it recertified the eastbound train engineer in 2009. In addition, according to notes in the UP's Health and Medical Services Encounters record for the eastbound engineer, the UP's chief medical officer determined after his conversation with the optometrist that the engineer would need retesting after 1 year. There is no evidence that the UP ever retested the engineer's visual acuity or obtained any further information regarding the engineer's vision. The UP's chief medical officer at the time is no longer employed by the UP and was not available for an interview with the NTSB. The NTSB concludes that the UP failed to adhere to its policy requiring written documentation from an outside source to verify visual acuity and failed to perform follow-up testing recommended by its own chief medical officer, either of which would have helped ensure that vision standards were continuously being met. Therefore, the NTSB recommends that the UP audit its medical records to ensure that all personnel in safety-sensitive positions have adequate documentation of appropriate medical testing.

1.6 Alternate Color Vision Field Test

In addition to failing initial visual acuity testing, the engineer of the eastbound train failed the Ishihara color vision test for the first time in 2009. Federal regulations in 49 CFR 240.121(e) permit locomotive engineers to retake vision tests when they fail to meet the standards for certification, with a limit on the number of retests permitted. The regulations allow the use of alternate color vision tests, such as one of several standardized color vision tests or an unspecified field or, practical, test. The choice of test is at the discretion of the railroad's chief medical examiner in consultation with the railroad's designated supervisor of locomotive engineers. According to the regulations, the railroad's medical examiner is expected to review all pertinent information and, under some circumstances, may restrict an examinee who does not meet the criteria from operating the train at night, during adverse weather conditions, or under other circumstances.

The engineer of the eastbound train was retested for color vision using the UP field test protocol on September 17, 2009. The UP field test instructions state that 10 wayside signal configurations will be presented to the examinee in a preselected order. The examinee is asked to stand at ground level, about 440 yards away from the signal mast. No measurement of the distance is required. One of the 10 possible signal configurations is dark/unlit. Scoring is performed by a supervisor, who follows a written protocol to record the approximate length of time the examinee takes to identify the lighted colors and interpret the meaning of each displayed signal (scored as 1–2 seconds, 2–3 seconds, and more than 3 seconds). However, no actual measurement of the time taken to perform this task is required. If any of the 10 signals is not displayed, the examiner must note the reason. No minimum number of signals is required by the UP's protocol.

Present at the time of the engineer's test were a supervisor administering the test and the engineer's labor representative. For the engineer's test, six signal configurations were presented (one configuration was dark) and the remaining four configurations were noted as being "unavailable." Thus, only 6 of 10 (60 percent) expected signal conditions were assessed in the engineer's color vision field test, and one of those was dark. According to UP medical records, the engineer passed the color vision field test on September 17, 2009, by identifying each of six wayside signal configurations within 1–2 seconds.

According to the current UP chief medical officer, the UP's test has been in use since 1999 and complies with 49 CFR Part 240, Appendix F, which regulates secondary color vision testing. However, he was unable to provide information on when, why, or by whom the color vision field test was developed. Moreover, he stated that the reliability and validity of the UP's color vision field test have not been evaluated, either by UP internal vision experts or by external vision experts. Therefore, the NTSB concludes that the UP routinely relies on a color vision field test of unknown validity, reliability, and comparability for medical certification of employees in safety-sensitive positions. Initially, the UP medical officer reported to the NTSB that enough crewmembers fail the primary color vision testing that the railroad performs secondary testing once or twice each month. However, the UP recently reported that it has administered this secondary color vision test 365 times since the beginning of 2008, and eight people were considered to have failed the exam. This equates to a 2.19 percent failure rate per test taken. However, the time period covers more than 3 years (the interval for medical certification exams); some of these engineers would have been tested twice. If the 365 tests were performed evenly over the time period, this would cover about 200 people (365 tests in 66 months with a requirement for retesting every 36 months). The actual failure rate of secondary testing is therefore likely to be closer to 4 percent per engineer tested. These 200 people who failed primary testing represent 1.4 percent of the 14,642 medically certified engineers at the UP.

Further, the test scoring sheet provides space for recording the test conditions: yard versus mainline track, approximate viewing distance (expected to be 440 yards), and ambient weather (dark, daylight, clear, cloudy, fog, rain, snow). The scoring sheet for the engineer's field test indicated that the test was conducted in a yard, at a viewing distance of 440 yards, and in daylight and clear weather. Although these conditions were reasonable, the field test does not evaluate a person's ability to accurately perceive signals under common but less than ideal situations, such as during adverse weather, after dark, or under glaring sun. Therefore, the NTSB concludes that the field test used by the UP fails to ensure that UP employees have adequate color perception to perform in safety-sensitive positions. The NTSB recommends that the UP replace its color vision field test with a test that has established and acceptable levels of validity, reliability, and comparability to ensure that certified employees in safety-sensitive positions have sufficient color discrimination to perform safely. The NTSB further recommends that until the UP has implemented a validated, reliable, and comparable color vision field test, the UP perform a safety analysis and undertake measures to manage the risk created by the use of an inadequate test. Such measures might include, but are not limited to, restricting crewmembers who have failed primary color vision testing to yard assignments or unsignaled territory. The NTSB also recommends that once the UP's replacement color vision field test is implemented, the UP retest all certified UP employees in safety-sensitive positions who failed the primary color vision testing on their last medical certification exam using the new procedure.

The color vision field tests used by the railroads vary widely. Amtrak requires that the supervisor conducting the field test has passed initial color testing (that is, has passed the Ishihara color plate test and did not require a field test) and is certified to perform the same job as the examinee. The Amtrak test is conducted under three lighting conditions including daylight, night, and dusk or dawn and at three distances, typically 1/16 mile (330 feet), 1/8 mile (660 feet), and 1/4 mile (1320 feet). For the Amtrak test, a minimum of 10 signals are presented in each of the three lighting and distance conditions, and the signal aspects are designed to emphasize those combinations with which the employee may be expected to have difficulty, based on results of their prior color vision testing. Examinees must describe and interpret each of the signals in less than 3 seconds. A single response delayed longer than 3 seconds or an incorrect response constitutes a failure of the color vision field test. If the employee is moved to a route where the signals are significantly different, a repeat color vision field test may be required. Similarly, the test used by CSX Transportation (CSX) requires evaluation both in daylight and at night; the CSX notes that "the ability to identify colors may be affected by lighting conditions." Additionally, the CSX test is performed on a moving train. The supervisor performing the evaluation notes the distance at which he can see and interpret the signals and the distance at which the examinee can see and interpret the signals. The CSX test instructions require that the evaluation is "of sufficient duration to enable observance of numerous signal aspects," but no minimum number is stated in the instructions. The supervisor then writes a recommendation indicating "whether the employee can or cannot properly identify signal aspects in time to safely comply with the signal indication." No scoring instructions are defined.

Although the federal regulations for secondary color vision tests (49 CFR Part 240, Appendix F) provide some flexibility in accommodating employees' circumstances or for adopting new test technologies, the lack of specificity in the regulations creates safety risks and opportunities for shortcomings in the visual test protocols. For example, the allowance for field tests creates opportunities for the use of nonstandard procedures with unknown diagnostic sensitivity, reliability, and validity. Also, because color vision is a critical safety capability needed by locomotive crewmembers, color vision tests must establish unequivocally that crewmembers can identify the colored aspects of wayside signals regardless of lighting and weather conditions. The federal regulations provide general guidance for administering color vision field tests but do not provide specific procedures, pass-fail criteria, or interpretation guidelines for these tests. In fact, the regulations allow enough discretion by an individual railroad that an engineer with limited color vision could fail one railroad's secondary testing (and be denied medical certification) but pass the secondary testing of another railroad. The NTSB therefore concludes that color vision field tests used after standardized color vision tests have been failed are not defined in FRA regulations to ensure valid, reliable, and comparable assessments. The NTSB recommends that the FRA determine what constitutes a valid, reliable, and comparable field test procedure for assessing the color discrimination capabilities of employees in safety-sensitive positions. When the FRA has made the determination in the previous safety recommendation, the NTSB recommends that the FRA require railroads to use a valid, reliable, and comparable field test procedure for assessing the color discrimination capabilities of employees in safety-sensitive positions.

1.7 Adequacy of Medical Evaluation of Train Crewmembers

According to 49 CFR 240.121(f), the engineer of the eastbound train had an obligation to report any further decline in his visual function to the railroad:

> As a condition of maintaining certification, each certified locomotive engineer shall notify his or her employing railroad's medical department or, if no such department exists, an appropriate railroad official if the person's best correctable vision or hearing has deteriorated to the extent that the person no longer meets one or more of the prescribed vision or hearing standards or requirements of this section. This notification is required prior to any subsequent operation of a locomotive or train which would require a certified locomotive engineer.

Further, according to UP Safety Rule 90.4, an employee is required to report any health changes by

> [n]otifying the supervisor when the employee becomes aware of or is concerned that a medical condition or symptom(s) exists which may affect his/her ability to safely perform his/her job. (UP 2010)

Once informed of a medical condition, the supervisor and the medical officer make a determination about safety and ability and either place the employee on leave, begin the temporary or permanent disability process, or terminate employment.

By August 2010, nearly a year after the eastbound train engineer first failed visual acuity and color vision testing, the engineer was complaining of difficulty seeing train signals, and formal color vision testing revealed severe protanopia. In addition, the engineer had his visual acuity measured by various eye-care providers six times in August and September 2010. Although the vision in the right eye was measured as acceptable (20/40) on one of these examinations, it was never measured as better than 20/80 in the left eye. The other measurements in the left eye ranged from 20/100 to 20/200. If the engineer had been reevaluated in 2010 as planned by the UP or after he self-reported his vision treatments and test results, it is unlikely that he would have continued to be medically certified and the collision may have been avoided.

The NTSB previously has encountered the problem of employees in safety-sensitive positions not reporting changes in their health status to railroads and has made a series of safety recommendations to address this issue. On February 9, 1996, about 8:40 a.m., two New Jersey Transit commuter trains collided nearly head-on in Secaucus, New Jersey (NTSB 1997b). About 400 passengers were on the trains; 3 people were killed and 158 were injured in the collision. The NTSB determined that the collision occurred because one train engineer failed to perceive a red signal aspect. The engineer had longstanding diabetes, which caused him to develop a color vision deficiency. He had not reported his diabetes to New Jersey Transit, but he was not required to do so under FRA regulations. As a result of that accident, the NTSB issued the following safety recommendations:

To the FRA:

> Require as a condition of certification that no person may act as an engineer with a known medical deficiency, or increase of a known medical deficiency, that would make that person unable to meet medical certification requirements. (R-97-2)

To New Jersey Transit:

> Inform your employees, especially those in safety-critical positions, of the facts and circumstances of this accident stressing that they must accurately report their use of medications or any changes in their medical condition. (R-97-4)

To AAR (R-97-5), Brotherhood of Locomotive Engineers (R-97-6), UTU (R-97-7), and American Public Transit Association (R-97-8):

> Provide your members with information about this accident, specifically explaining acquired vision deficiency and emphasizing the importance of ensuring the color vision requirement. Stress that railroad employees in safety sensitive positions, especially engineers, report their use of medications or any changes in their medical condition to their employer.

Safety Recommendations R-97-2 and -4 through -8 have been classified "Closed—Acceptable Action."

These NTSB safety recommendations led to changes in federal regulations and a number of improvements across the railroad industry that increased the awareness, monitoring, and regulation of medical conditions that affect human vision. New Jersey Transit improved its medical examinations for all locomotive engineers and increased the frequency of examinations for engineers with known medical conditions, such as diabetes, from annually to twice a year. The AAR, the Brotherhood of Locomotive Engineers, the UTU, and the American Public Transit Association undertook employee awareness campaigns to inform their members about the accident and the importance of self-reporting medical conditions that could affect their performance in safety-sensitive jobs. The FRA issued a final rule to revise 49 CFR Part 240 with enhanced qualifications and certification procedures for locomotive engineers. In particular, the FRA updated 49 CFR 240.121 by specifying a list of approved vision tests for the initial evaluation of the color vision. However, although some railroad companies perform more comprehensive medical evaluations and more frequent evaluations, the current regulations do not require anything other than vision and hearing testing every 3 years.

On November 15, 2001, two Canadian National/Illinois Central Railway trains collided near Clarkston, Michigan (NTSB 2002), killing two crewmembers and seriously injuring two other crewmembers. The NTSB investigation revealed that the two crewmembers who passed a stop signal had both been informed by their private physicians that they had potentially incapacitating medical conditions. Neither crewmember had informed the railroad, and neither had received sufficient treatment to mitigate the problem. The NTSB determined that the probable cause of the accident was the "crewmembers' fatigue, which was primarily due to the engineer's untreated and the conductor's insufficiently treated obstructive sleep apnea" (NTSB 2002). As a result of that accident, the NTSB issued the following safety recommendations to the FRA:

> Develop a standard medical examination form that includes questions regarding sleep problems and require that the form be used, pursuant to Title 49 *Code of Federal Regulations* Part 240, to determine the medical fitness of locomotive engineers; the form should also be available for use to determine the medical fitness of other employees in safety-sensitive positions. (R-02-24)

> Require that any medical condition that could incapacitate, or seriously impair the performance of, an employee in a safety-sensitive position be reported to the railroad in a timely manner. (R-02-25)

> Require that, when a railroad becomes aware that an employee in a safety-sensitive position has a potentially incapacitating or performance-impairing medical condition, the railroad prohibit that employee from performing any safety-sensitive duties until the railroad's designated physician determines that the employee can continue to work safely in a safety-sensitive position. (R-02-26)

In response to Safety Recommendation R-02-24, the FRA initiated a Railroad Safety Advisory Committee (RSAC) working group on medical standards to address the issues uncovered in the Clarkston accident. Because the FRA initially responded positively to the emerging public concerns about health issues in the railroad industry with research and regulatory work (FRA 2005), R-02-24 was classified "Open—Acceptable Response." However, the NTSB has monitored the RSAC medical standards group since its initiation and is aware that the RSAC has not proposed any new medical standards or educational materials, and the FRA has made no changes to improve the medical certification of railroad employees in safety-sensitive positions in the 11 years since the Clarkston accident. Moreover, the FRA has indicated that future products from the RSAC medical standards working group will be guidelines for the railroad industry, rather than information to support improved regulations.

The Goodwell accident is not the first since Clarkston where medical conditions that were not being monitored or evaluated by the railroad led to a train crew's failure to respond appropriately to wayside signals. On April 17, 2011, a BNSF Railway (BNSF) coal train collided with the rear end of a standing BNSF maintenance-of-way equipment train near Red Oak, Iowa (NTSB 2012). Both crewmembers in the striking locomotive were killed; both had met the FRA-required vision and hearing standards and were medically certified at the time. The engineer had been diagnosed with obesity, diabetes, hypertension, and high cholesterol. The conductor was obese and had been treated for restless leg syndrome, hypertension, and depression. Although both crewmembers had significant risk factors for sleep apnea, and the conductor had been treated for restless leg syndrome, neither had undergone a sleep study. Combined with irregular work hours, these medical conditions led to the crewmembers' falling asleep while operating the train, resulting in their failure to appropriately slow and stop their train following a restricted signal, with the readily visible equipment train on the track.

The FRA also has not adequately addressed Safety Recommendations R-02-25 and -26 resulting from the Clarkston accident. Although 49 CFR 240.121(f) requires employees to self-report deterioration in vision or hearing, there is no requirement that railroad employees in safety-sensitive positions report any other medical issue that might impair or affect their ability to operate a train safely. The RSAC working group on medical standards also has not made progress in the area addressed by Safety Recommendation R-02-26, which requires railroads to prohibit an employee known to have a potentially incapacitating or performance-impairing medical condition from performing any safety-sensitive duties until the railroad's designated physician determines that the employee can continue to work safely in a safety-sensitive position. The areas addressed by all three of these safety recommendations (R-02-24, -25, and -26) are discussed further later in this report.

Current FRA regulations place the onus of reporting new or deteriorating health concerns that could impair performance on the employee. This first presumes employees can successfully determine what constitutes a health concern that could impair their performance. As demonstrated in the Goodwell accident, the regulations place the onus on the employee even when the railroad knows that an employee has a chronic disease with the potential to dangerously deteriorate. In addition, both the Goodwell and the Clarkston accidents demonstrate that relying on employees to self-report to the railroad potentially dangerous medical conditions may not be optimal when there are potential financial and personal disincentives to reporting. This requirement may also be unrealistic because employees may not know whether they meet the standards.

While it continues to be the case that the only FRA requirements for crewmember medical certification are vision and hearing testing, other medical problems have contributed to serious train accidents. In Secaucus in 1996, the contributing medical problem was diabetes, which caused a color vision problem. In Clarkston in 2001, it was sleep apnea. In Red Oak in 2011, it was fatigue stemming from a combination of obesity, hypertension, diabetes, high cholesterol, a sleep disorder, and irregular work hours.

Among the four crewmembers involved in the Goodwell accident, three were obese at the time of their preemployment exams. Obesity is associated with developing sleep apnea, diabetes, hypertension, and high cholesterol. However, the UP never reevaluated the BMI of any of these employees. In addition to the eastbound engineer, who had vision problems, the conductor had mild hypertension according to his wife, and the westbound engineer had poorly controlled hypertension identified on a preemployment physical. The UP had no knowledge of the eastbound conductor's hypertension or any details relating to its treatment because it developed after his preemployment exam in 2003, and the UP never required another blood pressure measurement or list of medications. When the westbound engineer reported having hypertension at his new-hire physical in 1995, he was taking three medications for it. However, during the examination, his blood pressure was measured at 170/80. Normal blood pressure and well-controlled hypertension are below 140/90. The examining (outside) physician recommended that the engineer follow up with his primary care doctor about his hypertension. Over the next 17 years, no mention of blood pressure, its measurement, or its treatment was made anywhere in the westbound engineer's UP medical record. Hypertension, particularly when poorly controlled, is a common precursor of heart attacks, heart failure, kidney failure, strokes, and dementia. Any of these conditions could impair the safe operation of a train. Under current

FRA regulations, the UP was not required to perform any evaluation of height, weight, BMI, blood pressure, or medication use by any of these crewmembers.

Other federally regulated transportation modes have more comprehensive medical certification regulations. The Federal Aviation Administration (FAA) regulations, which cover about 600,000 commercial and private pilots, are at Title 14 CFR Part 67. The Federal Motor Carrier Safety Administration's (FMCSA) regulations governing the medical certification of more than 2.6 million drivers[22] are at Title 49 CFR Part 391 Subpart E. The US Coast Guard's regulations regarding medical certification of about 83,000 merchant mariners are at Title 46 CFR Part 10 Subpart B. With rare exceptions such as entry level ratings and shipboard food service workers, all these modes require a complete medical history, a list of medications, and a thorough physical exam for operators under their jurisdictions. Both the FAA and the FMCSA require the evaluation to be carried out by a trained and certified medical examiner (for the regulations requiring this, see Title 14 CFR Part 183 Subpart C for the FAA and Title 49 CFR Part 390 Subpart D for the FMCSA). All three transportation modes increase the frequency of medical evaluations for operators with identified chronic medical conditions that have the potential to worsen over time. For comparison, there are about 68,000 train engineer jobs in the United States.

The FAA issues three levels of medical certification, with a first-class certificate having the most stringent criteria. First-class medical certificates are mandatory for airline transport pilots exercising the privileges of their credentials by working for airlines, and they expire more quickly than second- or third-class certificates. For all classes, the interval between required examinations decreases after age 40.

For more than 30 years the FAA has used a system of special issuance medical certification that awards time-limited certification with specified retesting for pilots with medical conditions that have the potential to worsen over time. The FAA has listed specific medical conditions as disqualifying; finding these conditions during an initial medical certification examination requires the aviation medical examiner (AME) to defer certification to the FAA. At that time, further medical information and testing are required before the pilot can be certified. For many conditions that are otherwise disqualifying, when a special issuance is granted, the certificate is issued with a time limitation, usually restricting the validity of the medical certification to only 1 year. Specific follow-up evaluations must occur at specified intervals for each recertification.

For the FAA, glaucoma and hypertension are both specifically identified conditions requiring special attention. For glaucoma, after an initial special issuance, annual reissuance by an AME requires a pilot to provide the results of a series of specified tests performed by the pilot's ophthalmologist. Recertification by the AME may occur only if the pilot's ophthalmologist finds visual acuity at least at specified standards: 20/20 in each eye separately for a first- or second-class certificate and 20/40 in each eye separately for a third-class medical certificate. If at any time the pilot's visual acuity falls below these standards, the certification

---

[22] The covered motor vehicle operators are drivers of commercial vehicles operating interstate and above 10,001 pounds of gross vehicle weight or carrying more than eight passengers, and drivers of all vehicles requiring a commercial driver license (26,001 pounds or higher gross vehicle weight).

must be deferred and the pilot referred to the FAA for further evaluation of the pilot's fitness to fly (FAA 2013, 131). For hypertension, if the pilot is taking only specified classes of medication and the blood pressure measured by the AME is below 155/95, the pilot may be certified. Measured hypertension above this limit, as in the case of the westbound engineer in this collision, requires deferral of certification by the AME and further FAA evaluation.

Medical monitoring and reporting programs used in other transportation modes do not rely solely on the employee to self-report deterioration in chronic conditions. Instead, other modes have identified specific chronic conditions with the potential for deterioration and require more frequent, specified medical evaluation and certification for employees in safety-sensitive positions who have those conditions. The NTSB concludes that medical certification requirements identifying chronic conditions with the potential to deteriorate dangerously, such as glaucoma, and increased frequency of medical evaluation for those conditions would very likely have identified the further decline in the eastbound engineer's vision and would have decertified him prior to this accident. Therefore, the NTSB recommends that the FRA require more frequent medical certification exams for employees in safety-sensitive positions who have chronic conditions with the potential to deteriorate sufficiently to impair safe job performance.

The NTSB acknowledges that specific job requirements differ across various modes of transportation, leading to different occupational health standards. However, many of the safety risks created by health problems or their treatments are similar. The medical certification process used by the FAA requires a complete medical examination (rather than one limited to vision and hearing) (FAA 2013). Effective in 2014, the FMCSA is upgrading its process to authorize only specially trained and certified medical examiners to perform medical certification exams (*Federal Register* 2008, 73096). The Coast Guard is also exploring a similar program (*Federal Register* 2013, 19725).

In addition, each of these transportation modes incorporates central oversight of workers who have medical conditions that are initially disqualifying and require retesting, specialist evaluation, or medical determination that the condition does not impair the ability to perform safely. Each of these medical certification processes includes the ability to shorten the duration of certification when the condition has the potential to deteriorate. The exact requirements for evaluation depend on the condition but are clearly defined and consistent within each mode. Leaving such assessments to individual employers predictably results in different tests and test standards across the industry.

Both the FMCSA's current program change and the Coast Guard's potential change, if enacted, will bring medical certification for those modes into closer alignment with the FAA system. The NTSB concludes that upgrading FRA medical certification requirements for employees in safety-sensitive positions to include comprehensive health examinations, standardized testing across the industry, and centralized oversight of certification decisions when initial testing is failed, as well as more frequent medical certification when an employee has a condition with the potential to deteriorate, would improve transportation safety. Therefore, the NTSB recommends that the FRA develop medical certification regulations for employees in safety-sensitive positions that include, at a minimum, (1) a complete medical history that includes specific screening for sleep disorders, a review of current medications, and a thorough physical examination; (2) standardization of testing protocols across the industry; and

(3) centralized oversight of certification decisions for employees who fail initial testing; and consider requiring that medical examinations be performed by those with specific training and certification in evaluating medication use and health issues related to occupational safety on railroads. This recommendation supersedes three safety recommendations to the FRA: R-02-24, which requires the development of a medical examination form with questions about sleep problems for use in determining the medical fitness of locomotive engineers; R-02-25, which requires employees to report performance-impairing medical conditions to the railroad; and R-02-26, which requires a railroad to prohibit an employee from performing safety-sensitive duties if the railroad is aware that the employee has a performance-impairing medical condition. Therefore, Safety Recommendations R-02-24, -25, and -26, previously classified "Open—Acceptable Response," are now classified "Closed—Unacceptable Action/Superseded."

1.8 Locomotive Recorders

The eastbound train had four locomotives (three at the front of the train and one at the end of the train), and the westbound train had three locomotives (two at the front and one at the end). The lead locomotives of both trains had functionally integrated railroad equipment (FIRE) computers that recorded operating parameters, including those required by FRA regulations. These two locomotives also had certified crashworthy event recorder memory modules that received and recorded the data from the FIRE computer, even though such modules were not required.[23] In addition, the other five locomotives, which includes the trailing locomotives on both trains, had event recorders, but they were designed to capture only a limited set of parameters related to speed, throttle, and brakes, and they did not have certified crashworthy memory modules.[24]

Both trains had outward-facing locomotive-mounted video cameras on the lead and the trailing locomotives. After the collision, investigators recovered the video recorder from the westbound train's lead locomotive and the video recorders from the trailing locomotives of both trains. The video recorders were sent to the NTSB's Vehicle Recorder division for evaluation. The video recorder from the lead locomotive on the eastbound train was not recovered.

1.8.1 Event Recorders

After the collision, investigators were able to recover and download data from the event recorders from the trailing locomotives of both trains. Because of the extensive fire and collision damage to both lead locomotives, the FIRE computers on the lead locomotives were destroyed. Although the certified crashworthy event recorder memory modules from both lead locomotives were taken to the NTSB's Vehicle Recorder division for readout and evaluation, no data could be recovered from the severely damaged modules.

---

[23] According to a waiver approved by the FRA (*Federal Register* 2011b) AAR members (the UP is a member) are not required to have certified crashworthy event recorder memory modules until after the mandate of positive train control is effective, on December 31, 2015.

[24] The trailing locomotives did not have crew aboard and were controlled remotely by the engineer on the lead locomotive of each train.

Event Recorder Regulations. Since the 1970s, the NTSB has advocated the capture and preservation of onboard locomotive operational data to assist in accident investigations. After the NTSB's first recommendation on event recorders in 1978,[25] recorder and data storage technology improved, and railroads began to install locomotive event recorders in significantly greater numbers. By the 1990s, most railroads were installing event recorders on their locomotives. However, recorder data remained susceptible to damage during accidents, and the value of event recorders in accident investigations has been compromised in many cases.

In its investigation of a head-on collision between two UP freight trains in Devine, Texas, on June 22, 1997 (NTSB 1998), the NTSB found that the event recorders on both lead locomotives were destroyed and that critical operational data were lost. The NTSB made the following safety recommendation to the FRA:

> Working with the industry, develop and implement event recorder crashworthiness standards for all new or rebuilt locomotives by January 1, 2000. (R-98-30)

An FRA regulation requiring crashworthy event recorder memory modules was promulgated and became effective on October 1, 2005. The crashworthiness standards were to be phased in from 2006 to October 1, 2009, but with grandfathering and the AAR exemption, many locomotives may not have certified crashworthy event recorder memory modules for 20 or more years. In correspondence dated October 26, 2005, the NTSB stated its preference for stricter recorder survivability standards that would meet the European Organization for Civil Aviation Equipment standard. The NTSB noted that the regulatory standards issued by the FRA are less stringent. Nonetheless, the NTSB classified Safety Recommendation R-98-30 "Closed—Acceptable Action." The NTSB further noted that it would continue to monitor this situation and offer recommendations as a result of its (future) accident investigations to improve the effectiveness of crashworthiness standards and survivability of event recorders.

Unavailable Event Data. Although the NTSB successfully recovered data from the trailing locomotives' event recorders, the data those recorders captured were limited. The motion at the front of the trains, including the collision time and collision speeds, had to be calculated. The recorders on the lead locomotives were designed to capture many more parameters than the trailing locomotives' recorders. But because the lead locomotives' data modules were destroyed, despite their being certified crashworthy, important data were not available for analysis. For example, parameters recorded by the lead locomotives' recorders include those for alarms, the horn, and emergency brake applications, among others. Because these were not available to investigators, the investigation lacked critical information.

These critical data would be available for use by accident investigators if a redundant data set were recorded remote from the lead locomotives. For the Goodwell accident, locomotive speed data were available because they were stored in two locations: the lead and the trailing locomotives. The FRA should consider redundancy requirements to increase the likelihood of survivability of lead locomotive data in catastrophic accidents. This may include strategic

---

[25] Safety Recommendation R-78-44 to the FRA: Promulgate regulations to require locomotives used in trains on main tracks outside of yard limits to be equipped with operating event recorders. Classified "Closed—Unacceptable Action."

mounting locations for certified crashworthy event recorder memory modules (as far aft as practical), installation of more than one certified crashworthy memory module, data telemetry options to transmit data continuously from the lead locomotive to an alternate location on the train (such as the end-of-train device), or other redundant solutions that can increase the likelihood of data availability after an accident. Some railroads have made significant improvements in the capture of critical event recorder data. For example, Amtrak's Wi-Tronics system notifies railroad managers immediately anytime an Amtrak locomotive experiences an undesired emergency air brake application. When this occurs, the system also immediately transmits vital train data to a remote location, ensuring data redundancy.

Even though both lead locomotives had certified crashworthy memory modules, key event data were unrecoverable and, therefore, unavailable to investigators. With some key data stored on the trailing locomotives, which avoided the damage and fire from the collision, valuable data were retrieved, enabling NTSB investigators to reconstruct some of the events leading up to the accident to aid in the investigation. However, because only a portion of the important data were stored in more than one location, data critical to the investigation were destroyed in the collision and fire. The NTSB concludes that redundant storage of event data provided critical data to the accident investigation that would have been otherwise unavailable. The NTSB recommends that the FRA require all information captured by any required recorder to also be recorded in another location remote from the lead locomotive(s) to minimize the likelihood of the information's being unrecoverable as a result of an accident.

1.8.2 Video Recorders

The video recorders on the locomotives in the Goodwell accident were not required by regulation and were not protected from impact or fire. The video recorders from the trailing locomotives of both trains were undamaged and downloaded normally but provided limited information. The video recorder from the lead locomotive on the eastbound train was not recovered. The video recorder from the lead locomotive of the westbound train was severely damaged by fire. The enclosure was opened and inside were unrecognizable burned and broken small pieces of debris, dust, and ash. (See figure 7.)

Figure 7. Interior of video recorder hard drive enclosure from lead locomotive of westbound train.

Outward-facing video cameras are not required by regulation. However, some railroads are installing them to record conditions related to accidents involving pedestrians and highway-rail grade crossings. Both locomotives in the Goodwell, Oklahoma, accident and the lead locomotive in the April 17, 2011, Red Oak, Iowa, accident (NTSB 2012) had outward-facing video cameras. However, in both accidents, the video data were not available because the recorded data were not stored in crashworthy memory modules and were lost to collision and fire damage.

The NTSB believes that it would be a good safety practice for railroads to ensure that data from these cameras are safeguarded. The NTSB concludes that because data from locomotive video cameras are typically not stored in crashworthy memory modules, important operational and safety data are at risk of being lost after an accident. Addressing this risk provides an opportunity for the industry to revisit the best methods to preserve electronic data. In the Red Oak, Iowa, report, the NTSB made the following recommendation to the AAR:

> Develop a standard that specifies the use of suitable crash-protected memory modules for all new and existing installations of onboard video and audio recorders. The memory modules should meet or exceed the survivability criteria

specified in Title 49 *Code of Federal Regulations* Section 229.135, Appendix D, Table 2. (R-12-24) (NTSB 2012)

Because valuable information contained in the recorders was destroyed by the collision and subsequent fire in the Goodwell, Oklahoma, accident, the NTSB reiterates Safety Recommendation R-12-24 to the AAR and appreciates the work being done to develop the standard.

1.8.3 In-Cab Audio and Video Recordings

Since the late 1990s, the NTSB has recommended that the FRA require audio recorders inside locomotive cabs so that accident investigators can understand the actions of crewmembers just before an accident. As a result of the investigation of the collision between a Maryland Rail Commuter train and an Amtrak train near Silver Spring, Maryland, on February 16, 1996 (NTSB 1997a), in which no operating crewmembers survived, the NTSB was unable to determine whether crewmember activities leading up to the accident contributed to the accident. Consequently, the NTSB made the following safety recommendation to the FRA:

> Amend 49 *Code of Federal Regulations* Part 229 to require the recording of train crewmembers' voice communications for exclusive use in accident investigations and with appropriate limitations on the public release of such recordings. (R-97-9)

After the NTSB's investigation of a Bryan, Ohio, railroad accident that occurred in 1999 (NTSB 2001), with no surviving crewmembers, the NTSB reiterated this safety recommendation. The FRA responded that it

> … has reluctantly come to the conclusion that this recommendation should not be implemented at the present time. … [The] FRA appreciates that, as time passes and other uses are found for recording media that may create synergies with other public and private purposes, the [NTSB's] recommendation may warrant re-examination.

Based on this response and further meetings, the NTSB classified Safety Recommendation R-97-9 "Closed—Unacceptable Action."

Since the refusal by the FRA to act on the recommendation of in-cab recorders, the NTSB has continued to investigate accidents in which audio recorders, along with video recorders, would have provided valuable information to help determine probable cause and develop safety recommendations. These include the July 10, 2005, collision of two Canadian National Railroad (CN) freight trains in Anding, Mississippi (NTSB 2007), after which the NTSB made the following safety recommendation to the FRA:

> Require the installation of a crash- and fire-protected locomotive cab voice recorder, or a combined voice and video recorder, (for the exclusive use in accident investigations and with appropriate limitations on the public release of such recordings) in all controlling locomotive cabs and cab car operating compartments. The recorder should have a minimum 2-hour continuous recording

capability, microphones capable of capturing crewmembers' voices and sounds generated within the cab, and a channel to record all radio conversations to and from crewmembers. (R-07-3)

The NTSB has found that in many accidents, the individuals involved either have limited recollection of events or, as at Goodwell, were killed in the accident. In the September 12, 2008, railroad accident in Chatsworth, California (NTSB 2010), a westbound Southern California Regional Rail Authority Metrolink train collided head-on with an eastbound UP freight train, resulting in 25 fatalities, including the engineer of the Metrolink train, and 101 injuries. For many accidents the NTSB has investigated, a better knowledge of crewmembers' actions before the accident would have helped reveal key causal factors and facilitated the development of more effective safety recommendations. In the Goodwell accident, video could have shed light on the activities of the crew of the eastbound train leading up to the collision and why the crew did not respond to wayside signals.

The NTSB believes that the only reasonable and reliable mechanism for making such observations is an in-cab audio and image recorder that would capture crewmembers' activities while in the train operating compartment. As a result of the investigation of the Chatsworth accident, the NTSB made two safety recommendations to the FRA:

> Require the installation, in all controlling locomotive cabs and cab car operating compartments, of crash- and fire-protected inward- and outward-facing audio and image recorders capable of providing recordings to verify that train crew actions are in accordance with rules and procedures that are essential to safety as well as train operating conditions. The devices should have a minimum 12-hour continuous recording capability with recordings that are easily accessible for review, with appropriate limitations on public release, for the investigation of accidents or for use by management in carrying out efficiency testing and systemwide performance monitoring programs. (R-10-1)

The NTSB reclassified Safety Recommendation R-07-3 "Closed—Unacceptable Action/Superseded" when it issued Safety Recommendation R-10-1 to the FRA. The NTSB also issued the following safety recommendation to the FRA:

> Require that railroads regularly review and use in-cab audio and image recordings (with appropriate limitations on public release), in conjunction with other performance data, to verify that train crew actions are in accordance with rules and procedures that are essential to safety. (R-10-2)

The FRA has acknowledged the value of using audio and imaging technology in locomotives and cab cars; however, it has not taken action to implement the safety recommendations. Until the FRA requires that locomotives and cab cars operated under 49 CFR Part 229 be equipped with crash- and fire-protected inward-facing audio and image recorders, Safety Recommendations R-10-1 and -2 are classified "Open—Unacceptable Response."

The NTSB is concerned that the lack of action by the FRA leaves many safety lessons unlearned and thereby unnecessarily delays improvements in the safe operation of railroads.

Until the actions of crewmembers during train operations can be meaningfully monitored, the NTSB recognizes that opportunities will be missed to understand and improve safety after some accidents, and the missed opportunities are not infrequent, as discussed below.

The rear-end collision of two BNSF trains near Red Oak, Iowa, on April 17, 2011, again demonstrated the need for in-cab recording devices to better understand (and thereby help to prevent) serious railroad accidents that claim the lives of crewmembers, passengers, and the public. In the report on this accident, the NTSB stated that "while video recorders will assist in the investigation of accidents, their value in preventing accidents cannot be overstated" (NTSB 2012) and added that the installation of inward-facing cameras could also assist railroads in monitoring rules compliance and identifying fatigued engineers, which could lead to interventions that could prevent accidents.

During the Red Oak accident investigation, NTSB investigators determined, based on medical records, work-rest histories, and event recorder data from the lead locomotive, that the crewmembers of the striking coal train had fallen asleep just before the collision. However, without visual evidence of the crewmembers' actions during the trip, additional information about the crewmembers' performance was not available for investigators. In that accident, the NTSB concluded that "had an inward-facing video and audio recorder been installed in the cab of the locomotive of the striking train, additional valuable information about the train crew's actions before the collision would have been available" (NTSB 2012).

Also, in its report on the May 24, 2011, collision of two CSX trains in Mineral Springs, North Carolina (NTSB 2013a), the NTSB stated it was unable to determine why the crew of the striking train failed to comply with a wayside signal, because the crewmembers had been killed and the cab was not equipped with either an inward-facing camera or an audio recorder. The NTSB cannot develop effective recommendations to improve safety when critical elements of information are unavailable to the investigation.

In its recent report on the September 30, 2010, collision of two CN trains in Two Harbors, Minnesota, the NTSB noted that appropriate action had not been taken in response to Safety Recommendations R-10-1 and -2 (NTSB 2013b). In the investigation, investigators found that crewmembers of both trains had used cell phones in moving locomotives—a violation of railroad rules and FRA regulations. Moreover, the NTSB urged the FRA to "promptly initiate rulemaking activity for the audio and imaging requirements outlined in Safety Recommendations R-10-1 and -2" (NTSB 2013b) and reiterated these two safety recommendations, noting that FRA action on the recommendations would require locomotive manufacturers to implement important safety improvements. In the Two Harbors, Minnesota, accident report, the NTSB reiterated Safety Recommendations R-10-1 and -2, stating the following:

> The NTSB is disappointed that more than four years after the deadliest passenger train accident in decades, the FRA has not acted on two recommendations that would protect railroad employees, as well as the public. (NTSB 2013b)

The NTSB railroad accident investigations conducted since the issuance of Safety Recommendations R-10-1 and -2 consistently indicate that in-cab audio and video recorders could provide critical information for accident investigations about crew performance and the locomotive cab environment. The Goodwell accident demonstrates clearly that in-cab audio and video data, if sufficiently protected from fire and crash damage, could have provided information for understanding the actions of the crew of the eastbound train. Therefore, the NTSB reiterates Safety Recommendations R-10-1 and -2 to the FRA.

In its most recent response to the NTSB about Safety Recommendations R-10-1 and -2, on July 31, 2012, the FRA stated that it recognizes the inherent safety value of in-cab cameras and voice recordings for use in accident investigations. However, the FRA also stated that it is aware of "significant privacy concerns" among railroad employees; more specifically, the FRA stated that it fears that implementing Safety Recommendations R-10-1 and -2 might erode railroad employee morale, because some employees suspect that inward-facing cameras and voice recordings might be used for selective enforcement and retaliation by railroad management. Although the importance of management-labor relations is understood, the NTSB has based the two safety recommendations on objective and recurring evidence of significant risks to the safety of railroad employees and the public. Moreover, these safety risks are recognized within the railroad industry itself. The NTSB is aware that the Kansas City Southern Railway Company (KCSR), a Class I freight railroad, expressed intent on April 24, 2013, to install inward-facing cameras into its U.S. locomotives to improve its operational safety by reducing and mitigating the risks of human performance errors in locomotive cabs during train movements. The KCSR has encountered resistance to implementing its plan from two railroad labor unions, the BLET and the UTU, in the U.S. District Court for the Western District of Louisiana, Shreveport Division (Civil Action No. 5:13-cv-838); the case has not yet been resolved. The NTSB is pleased by the proactive initiative of the KCSR to implement inward-facing cameras and recognizes that the inherent safety value of inward-facing cameras and audio recorders applies equally to other Class I freight railroads. Therefore, the NTSB recommends that all Class I railroads install in all controlling locomotive cabs and cab car operating compartments crash- and fire-protected inward- and outward-facing audio and image recorders. The devices should have a minimum 12-hour continuous recording capability.

1.9 Positive Train Control

In the NTSB's nearly 50 years of investigating railroad accidents, including hundreds of train collisions and overspeed derailments, accidents have been caused by mechanical defects, maintenance issues, and track failures. However, the biggest safety challenge is human error, which is an area where technology can be very helpful. Since 2005, the NTSB has completed 16 investigations of railroad accidents that could have been prevented or mitigated with positive train control (PTC). These 16 accidents claimed 52 lives and injured 942 more; the damages totaled hundreds of millions of dollars. In each of these accidents, the NTSB concluded that PTC would have provided critical redundancy that would have prevented the accident. Had such a system been in place where the Goodwell accident occurred, it would have intervened when the eastbound train engineer failed to slow and ultimately stop his train at the red stop signal at the east end of the Goodwell siding.

Although human error cannot be completely eradicated, PTC technology is capable of supplementing the human operation of trains. Such systems provide a safety redundancy by slowing or stopping a train that is not being operated in accordance with signal systems and operating rules, as was the case in each of the 16 accidents referenced above. For years, PTC has been in place on Amtrak trains in the Northeast and Michigan, but for PTC to reach its greatest safety potential, it must be widely implemented across the United States.

Because of the NTSB's repeated findings that technology-based collision avoidance systems could provide the needed safety redundancy to prevent rail accidents, PTC was placed on the NTSB's Most Wanted List at the inception of that list in 1990. Following the tragic head-on collision between a passenger train and a freight train in Chatsworth, California, on September 12, 2008, which resulted in 25 fatalities and more than 100 injuries, Congress enacted the Rail Safety Improvement Act of 2008 (RSIA). This law requires each Class I railroad over which poisonous-by-inhalation or toxic-by-inhalation hazardous materials are transported and regularly scheduled intercity or commuter rail passenger transportation travels to implement a PTC system by December 31, 2015. Encouraged by this legislative action, the NTSB's safety recommendation calling for PTC to be installed on railroads was classified as closed and was removed from the Most Wanted List in October 2008. As a result of the May 2011 rear-end collision between two CSX freight trains in Mineral Springs, North Carolina, and the collision of the two UP trains in Goodwell, Oklahoma, the NTSB added PTC to the 2013 Most Wanted List.

The NTSB has long advocated the implementation of PTC systems to prevent train-to-train collisions. NTSB railroad accident investigations over the past 40 years have shown conclusively that the most effective way to avoid train-to-train collisions is through the use of PTC systems that will automatically assume some control of a train when the train crew does not comply with the requirements of a signal indication. Had such a system been in place where this accident occurred, it would have intervened when the eastbound train engineer failed to slow and ultimately stop his train at the red stop signal at the east end of the Goodwell siding.

No PTC speed enforcement or stop-signal enforcement is installed in the area where this accident occurred. The UP is in the process of developing a PTC system, which would have prevented this accident if it had been in operation. In a test lab, NTSB investigators simulated the UP's proposed PTC system based on preliminary versions and using the current configuration of PTC software, simulators, and track profile data. In this testing, a train with characteristics similar to those of the eastbound train approached the stop signal at the east end of the siding at Goodwell, Oklahoma, using the downloaded event recorder data. The screen in the engine of the eastbound train would have displayed the following as the train progressed down the track:

- When the lead locomotive was near MP 487.8, the PTC system would have displayed a required stop for the signal at the east end of the siding (MP 483.7).

- When the lead locomotive was at MP 487.4, the PTC system would have provided to the train crew visual and audible warnings of a pending enforcement of the required stop.

- The PTC system would have continued to provide visual warning to the train crew for about 75 seconds.

- When the lead locomotive was near MP 485.7, the PTC system would have invoked a full-service enforcement brake application.

- When the lead locomotive was near MP 484.6, the brake application would have stopped the train.

The NTSB concludes that had a PTC system been installed and used on the UP's Pratt subdivision, this accident would have been prevented.

The RSIA mandated that not later than 18 months from the date of enactment, Class I railroads shall develop and submit to the Secretary of Transportation a plan for implementing a positive train control system by December 15, 2015. The plans were due on April 1, 2010, 18 months after the October 1, 2008, enactment date. This mandate applies to the UP track in the accident area. However, progress in the implementation of PTC systems has been slow.

1.9.1 Positive Train Control Forum

On February 27, 2013, the NTSB held a forum: "Positive Train Control: Is it on Track?"[26] This forum included three panels that addressed three broad issues:

- **PTC Systems as Envisioned vs. Implemented:** The panelists were Grady Cothen, Independent Transportation Consultant; Steven Ditmeyer, Independent Transportation Consultant; Mark Hartong, Ph.D., Senior Scientist and Technical Advisor for Railroad Electronics, FRA; and Gerhard Thelen, Vice President for Operation and Planning, Norfolk Southern, AAR.

- **Current Status of PTC Regulatory Implementation:** The panelists were David Blackmore, Program Manager for Applied Technologies, PTC Specialist, FRA; Frank Lanegro, Vice President of Mechanical, CSX, AAR; Lou Sanders, Director of Technical Services, American Public Transportation Association; Tom Schnautz, President, PTC-220;[27] Mark Hartong, Ph.D., Senior Scientist and Technical Advisor for Railroad Electronics, FRA; and Richard Arsenault, Chief Counsel, Mobility Division, Federal Communications Commission (FCC).

- **Current Status of PTC Technical Implementation**: The panelists were Jeffrey Young, PTC Program Manager, UP, AAR; Keith Holt, Deputy Chief Engineer, C&S Amtrak; Mike Baldwin, Director of Research, Brotherhood of Railroad Signalmen; Steven Bruno, Vice President, BLET; Frank Wilson, Wabtec; and Darell Maxey, Metrolink.

During the PTC forum, representatives from Norfolk Southern, the UP, and the AAR talked about the issues they had regarding the availability of radio frequency spectrum for use in

---

[26] Information about this forum is available at <http://www.ntsb.gov/news/events/2013/ptc/index.html>.

[27] PTC-220 is a spectrum holding company formed in 2007 that has the seven Class I freight railroads as members.

PTC systems. Responding to those issues was Richard Arsenault from the FCC. He stated that the FCC issued a public notice to ascertain spectrum needs for PTC, and he discussed the status of spectrum acquisition of some of the transit agencies. He stated that the Metropolitan Transportation Authority has more spectrum than it needs for PTC, with the exception of an area in Connecticut where the agency is still trying to resolve some remaining issues. Mr. Arsenault said that Long Island Railroad has more than adequate spectrum. Southeast Pennsylvania Transit Authority has already acquired the spectrum it needs and will provide some spectrum to New Jersey Transit. Southern California Regional Rail Authority has entered into a leasing arrangement with PTC-220 that was approved by the FCC. Mr. Arsenault said he had met in Chicago with Amtrak, commuter railroads, and PTC-220 to work together to solve any problems they may encounter, noting that Chicago is a good example of how to get the spectrum issue resolved. PTC-220 and Meteorcomm[28] have told the FCC that they have software that will enable PTC deployment efficiently and effectively. Mr. Arsenault concluded by telling the rail systems in attendance that if they find an entity that is not responsive to their spectrum needs, the FCC is ready to assist in any way necessary to help solve PTC spectrum problems (NTSB 2013d, 95–98).

Throughout the forum, panelists were asked whether their railroads were going to meet the date for PTC implementation stated in the RSIA. Jeff Young, PTC Program Manager for the UP, said that UP management did not expect implementation to be complete by the mandated 2015 date (NTSB 2013d, 141). He stated further that the railroad expects PTC system certification sometime in late 2014 and the system to be approved by the FRA by 2015 (NTSB 2013d, 142). Panelists were reminded that the RSIA was passed into law by Congress in October 2008, and the 2015 implementation date gave the railroads 7 years of lead time to complete PTC implementation (NTSB 2013d, 187). Gerhard Thelen from Norfolk Southern said the railroad likely would not have its PTC system fully implemented until between 2018 and 2020 (NTSB 2013d, 61). Instead of 7 years of lead time for PTC implementation, this would almost double the time to 12 years.

Congress has not waived or extended the December 31, 2015, date for PTC implementation. If a railroad fails to meet the statutory requirements of the RSIA, Appendix A to 49 CFR Part 236 lists the penalties for various violations. For failure to complete a PTC system installation on a track segment where PTC is required prior to December 31, 2015, (Section 236.1005) the penalty is $16,000. The penalty for operating a controlling locomotive in PTC territory without a required and operative PTC onboard apparatus (Section 236.1006) is $15,000. The penalty for failure to report the progress toward achieving the railroad's goal to deploy PTC and equip locomotives on PTC lines is $5,000. The penalty for operation of unequipped trains in PTC territory is $15,000. Every day beyond December 31, 2015, that a railroad fails to comply with the PTC requirements of the RSIA is a failure to meet the requirement. If Congress were to delay the statutory deadline, railroads that had delayed planning PTC implementation would be rewarded and railroads that had moved ahead with planning for PTC implementation by the deadline would essentially be punished. Therefore if Congress were to delay the deadline, the NTSB would encourage the FRA to adjust Appendix A to Part 236 accordingly. However if

---

[28] Meteorcomm is a provider of equipment and services to track, monitor, and control mobile and fixed assets for the railroad industry.

Congress does not delay the statutory deadline, the NTSB would encourage the FRA to use its regulatory authority to levy the appropriate penalties for all instances of noncompliance.

The PTC forum revealed that some railroads are working aggressively toward meeting the 2015 PTC implementation date. When asked specifically, Dr. Hartong of the FRA responded that Amtrak, Alaska Railroad, BNSF, and Metrolink had given every indication that they expect to complete PTC implementation by the 2015 date or earlier (NTSB 2013d, 99).

The Amtrak representative spoke about the challenges that his railroad faces with PTC implementation. In a related issue, on December 20, 2012, the FRA issued a report, *Railroad Safety: Amtrak Has Made Progress in Implementing Positive Train Control, but Significant Challenges Remain* (FRA 2012). This report discussed many PTC-related issues and made recommendations to Amtrak, including the following three:

- develop a master project schedule that includes detailed tasks and dependencies and periodically revise it;

- remain engaged with [the] FRA to increase the likelihood that the FRA review process stays on schedule; and

- engage sufficiently at the appropriate level with host railroads and others in the industry to influence developments with I-ETMS [Interoperable Electronic Train Management System] that affect Amtrak.

During the PTC forum, NTSB Board Members asked who is overseeing the timelines and milestones for overall PTC implementation and progress, where is that information kept, and is it accessible to the public?

In response, Dr. Hartong from the FRA said that the FRA continues to monitor progress for each railroad in the PTC implementation plan, as required. However, he added that there is no general oversight of implementation, and each railroad is responsible for its own plan (NTSB 2013d, 62–64). Although railroads appear to be making slow progress toward PTC implementation, the PTC forum made clear that an overall timeline and milestones do not exist, and that data on the railroads' progress toward PTC implementation are neither transparent nor available to the public.

During the PTC forum many railroad representatives stated that their railroads could not achieve PTC implementation by the 2015 date contained in the RSIA, but they provided no details of their progress to date or their overall implementation plans. The NTSB therefore concludes that if all railroads required to implement PTC provided frequent updates to the FRA on the progress of PTC implementation, the FRA and the public would be better able to follow the progress and estimate when railroads will come into compliance with the mandates in the RSIA. Therefore, the NTSB recommends that all railroads subject to the PTC provisions of the RSIA provide PTC implementation update reports to the FRA every 6 months until PTC implementation is complete. The update reports should consist of two sections: components and training. The components section should include a description of the PTC component to be implemented, the number of components, the number of components completed on the report date, the number of components that remain to be completed, the overall completion percentage, and the estimated completion date. Components are defined as locomotives, wayside units, switches, base station radios, wayside radios, locomotive radios, and any new and novel technologies that are part of a PTC system. The training section should include the number of safety-related employees and equivalent railroad carrier contractors and subcontractors that need to be trained, by class and craft; minimum training standards for those employees and contractors, meaning the knowledge of and ability to comply with federal railroad safety laws and regulations and carrier rules and procedures to implement PTC; the percentage of employees who have completed training; the percentage of employees who remain to be trained; and the estimated date that training will be completed. The NTSB further recommends that the FRA publish the PTC implementation update reports submitted by all railroads subject to the PTC provisions of the RSIA and make the reports available on the FRA website within 30 days of report receipt.

2 Conclusions

2.1 Findings

1. The following were not factors in the accident: the weather; the condition of the track, the locomotives, or the railcars; the signal system; cell phone use by any of the crewmembers; or drug or alcohol use by the conductor of the westbound train.

2. For undetermined reasons the conductor of the eastbound train was disengaged from performing his duties as the train passed the advance approach, approach, and stop signals.

3. Both crewmembers of the eastbound train failed to maintain proper crew coordination and jointly failed to make proper decisions and actions to control the train safely.

4. There is an adequate foundation of guidance and opportunity for railroads to develop and deploy crew resource management programs.

5. Had crewmembers of the eastbound train received training in and practiced the principles of crew resource management, they likely would have demonstrated improved coordination, communication, and discipline while operating the train.

6. A nonpunitive peer audit program is an important element of an effective safety management system and would provide railroads with opportunities to better understand and address operational safety issues.

7. Had the Union Pacific Railroad established, maintained, and enforced a safety management system, it is likely that this accident may have been avoided.

8. Insufficient information was available to determine whether fatigue of the eastbound crew was a factor in the accident.

9. The results from required medical examinations and Union Pacific Railroad conversations with the engineer's health care providers demonstrated to the Union Pacific Railroad that the eastbound train engineer's vision had significantly deteriorated because of a chronic medical condition.

10. The engineer of the eastbound train was unable to visually detect and correctly interpret the wayside signals.

11. The Union Pacific Railroad failed to adhere to its policy requiring written documentation from an outside source to verify visual acuity and failed to perform follow-up testing recommended by its own chief medical officer, either of which would have helped ensure that vision standards were continuously being met.

12. The Union Pacific Railroad routinely relies on a color vision field test of unknown validity, reliability, and comparability for medical certification of employees in safety-sensitive positions.

13. The field test used by the Union Pacific Railroad fails to ensure that Union Pacific Railroad employees have adequate color perception to perform in safety-sensitive positions.

14. Color vision field tests used after standardized color vision tests have been failed are not defined in Federal Railroad Administration regulations to ensure valid, reliable, and comparable assessments.

15. Medical certification requirements identifying chronic conditions with the potential to deteriorate dangerously, such as glaucoma, and increased frequency of medical evaluation for those conditions would very likely have identified the further decline in the eastbound engineer's vision and would have decertified him prior to this accident.

16. Upgrading Federal Railroad Administration medical certification requirements for employees in safety-sensitive positions to include comprehensive health examinations, standardized testing across the industry, and centralized oversight of certification decisions when initial testing is failed, as well as more frequent medical certification when an employee has a condition with the potential to deteriorate, would improve transportation safety.

17. Redundant storage of event data provided critical data to the accident investigation that would have been otherwise unavailable.

18. Because data from locomotive video cameras are typically not stored in crashworthy memory modules, important operational and safety data are at risk of being lost after an accident.

19. Had a positive train control system been installed and used on the Union Pacific Railroad's Pratt subdivision, this accident would have been prevented.

20. If all railroads required to implement positive train control provided frequent updates to the Federal Railroad Administration on the progress of positive train control implementation, the Federal Railroad Administration and the public would be better able to follow the progress and estimate when railroads will come into compliance with the mandates in the Rail Safety Improvement Act of 2008.

2.2 Probable Cause

The National Transportation Safety Board determines that the probable cause of this accident was the eastbound Union Pacific Railroad train crew's lack of response to wayside signals because of the engineer's inability to see and correctly interpret the signals; the conductor's disengagement from his duties; and the lack of positive train control, which would have stopped the train and prevented the collision regardless of the crew's inaction. Contributing to the accident was a medical examination process that failed to decertify the engineer before his deteriorating vision adversely affected his ability to operate a train safely.

3 Recommendations

3.1 New Recommendations

As a result of this investigation, the National Transportation Safety Board makes the following new safety recommendations:

To the Federal Railroad Administration:

Determine what constitutes a valid, reliable, and comparable field test procedure for assessing the color discrimination capabilities of employees in safety-sensitive positions. (R-13-18)

When you have made the determination in Safety Recommendation R-13-18, require railroads to use a valid, reliable, and comparable field test procedure for assessing the color discrimination capabilities of employees in safety-sensitive positions. (R-13-19)

Require more frequent medical certification exams for employees in safety-sensitive positions who have chronic conditions with the potential to deteriorate sufficiently to impair safe job performance. (R-13-20)

Develop medical certification regulations for employees in safety-sensitive positions that include, at a minimum, (1) a complete medical history that includes specific screening for sleep disorders, a review of current medications, and a thorough physical examination; (2) standardization of testing protocols across the industry; and (3) centralized oversight of certification decisions for employees who fail initial testing; and consider requiring that medical examinations be performed by those with specific training and certification in evaluating medication use and health issues related to occupational safety on railroads. (R-13-21)

Require all information captured by any required recorder to also be recorded in another location remote from the lead locomotive(s) to minimize the likelihood of the information's being unrecoverable as a result of an accident. (R-13-22)

Publish the positive train control implementation update reports submitted by all railroads subject to the positive train control provisions of the Rail Safety Improvement Act of 2008 and make the reports available on your website within 30 days of report receipt. (R-13-23)

To the Brotherhood of Locomotive Engineers and Trainmen:

Work with the Union Pacific Railroad and the United Transportation Union to develop and implement a nonpunitive peer audit program focused on rule compliance and operational safety for the Union Pacific Railroad. (R-13-24)

To the United Transportation Union:

Work with the Union Pacific Railroad and the Brotherhood of Locomotive Engineers and Trainmen to develop and implement a nonpunitive peer audit program focused on rule compliance and operational safety for the Union Pacific Railroad. (R-13-25)

To All Class I Railroads:

Install in all controlling locomotive cabs and cab car operating compartments crash- and fire-protected inward- and outward-facing audio and image recorders. The devices should have a minimum 12-hour continuous recording capability. (R-13-26)

To All Railroads Subject to the Positive Train Control Provisions of the Rail Safety Improvement Act of 2008:

Provide positive train control implementation update reports to the Federal Railroad Administration every 6 months until positive train control implementation is complete. The update reports should consist of two sections: components and training. The components section should include a description of the positive train control component to be implemented, the number of components, the number of components completed on the report date, the number of components that remain to be completed, the overall completion percentage, and the estimated completion date. Components are defined as locomotives, wayside units, switches, base station radios, wayside radios, locomotive radios, and any new and novel technologies that are part of a positive train control system. The training section should include the number of safety-related employees and equivalent railroad carrier contractors and subcontractors that need to be trained, by class and craft; minimum training standards for those employees and contractors, meaning the knowledge of and ability to comply with federal railroad safety laws and regulations and carrier rules and procedures to implement positive train control; the percentage of employees who have completed training; the percentage of employees who remain to be trained; and the estimated date that training will be completed. (R-13-27)

To Union Pacific Railroad:

Work with the Brotherhood of Locomotive Engineers and Trainmen and the United Transportation Union to develop and implement a nonpunitive peer audit program focused on rule compliance and operational safety. (R-13-28)

Develop and implement a plan to establish a safety management system, which incorporates crew resource management. (R-13-29)

Audit your medical records to ensure that all personnel in safety-sensitive positions have adequate documentation of appropriate medical testing. (R-13-30)

Replace your color vision field test with a test that has established and acceptable levels of validity, reliability, and comparability to ensure that certified employees in safety-sensitive positions have sufficient color discrimination to perform safely. (R-13-31)

Until you have implemented a validated, reliable, and comparable color vision field test, perform a safety analysis and undertake measures to manage the risk created by the use of an inadequate test. Such measures might include, but are not limited to, restricting crewmembers who have failed primary color vision testing to yard assignments or unsignaled territory. (R-13-32)

Once your replacement color vision field test is implemented, retest all certified Union Pacific Railroad employees in safety-sensitive positions who failed the primary color vision testing on their last medical certification exam using the new procedure. (R-13-33)

3.2 Previously Issued Recommendations Reiterated in this Report

As a result of this accident investigation, the National Transportation Safety Board reiterates the following previously issued safety recommendations:

To the Federal Railroad Administration:

Require the installation, in all controlling locomotive cabs and cab car operating compartments, of crash- and fire-protected inward- and outward-facing audio and image recorders capable of providing recordings to verify that train crew actions are in accordance with rules and procedures that are essential to safety as well as train operating conditions. The devices should have a minimum 12-hour continuous recording capability with recordings that are easily accessible for review, with appropriate limitations on public release, for the investigation of accidents or for use by management in carrying out efficiency testing and systemwide performance monitoring programs. (R-10-1 classified "Open—Unacceptable Response")

Require that railroads regularly review and use in-cab audio and image recordings (with appropriate limitations on public release), in conjunction with other performance data, to verify that train crew actions are in accordance with rules and procedures that are essential to safety. (R-10-2 classified "Open—Unacceptable Response")

To the Association of American Railroads:

Develop a standard that specifies the use of suitable crash-protected memory modules for all new and existing installations of onboard video and audio recorders. The memory modules should meet or exceed the survivability criteria specified in Title 49 *Code of Federal Regulations* Section 229.135, Appendix D, Table 2. (R-12-24 classified "Open—Initial Response Received")

3.3 Previously Issued Recommendations Reclassified in This Report

As a result of this accident investigation, the National Transportation Safety Board reclassifies from "Open—Acceptable Response" to "Closed—Unacceptable Action/Superseded," by Safety Recommendation R-13-21, the following safety recommendations to the Federal Railroad Administration:

Develop a standard medical examination form that includes questions regarding sleep problems and require that the form be used, pursuant to Title 49 *Code of Federal Regulations* Part 240, to determine the medical fitness of locomotive engineers; the form should also be available for use to determine the medical fitness of other employees in safety-sensitive positions. (R-02-24)

Require that any medical condition that could incapacitate, or seriously impair the performance of, an employee in a safety-sensitive position be reported to the railroad in a timely manner. (R-02-25)

Require that, when a railroad becomes aware that an employee in a safety-sensitive position has a potentially incapacitating or performance-impairing medical condition, the railroad prohibit that employee from performing any safety-sensitive duties until the railroad's designated physician determines that the employee can continue to work safely in a safety-sensitive position. (R-02-26)

BY THE NATIONAL TRANSPORTATION SAFETY BOARD

DEBORAH A.P. HERSMAN
Chairman

ROBERT L. SUMWALT
Member

CHRISTOPHER A. HART
Vice Chairman

MARK R. ROSEKIND
Member

EARL F. WEENER
Member

Adopted: June 18, 2013

Vice Chairman Hart filed the following concurring statement on June 24, 2013; Member Weener filed the following concurring statement on June 20, 2013.

Board Member Statements

Vice Chairman Christopher A. Hart, concurring

I concur with the findings, probable cause, and recommendations in this accident report, but I would like to address an ancillary issue that came to my attention as a result of the investigation of this accident – namely, that reports about running red signals are excluded from the protections of the FRA's Confidential Close Call Reporting System (C^3RS).

The railroad industry, to its credit, has created a near-miss reporting program, the C^3RS. Near-miss reporting programs have been very successful in other industries, most notably in aviation. Among the objectives of near-miss reporting programs are (a) providing a source of information about things that almost went wrong or almost resulted in a mishap, and (b) providing information about <u>why</u> something almost went wrong or almost resulted in a mishap. The first objective can be very important, especially if the near-miss reporting program is the only source of information about something that went wrong; but the second objective is <u>always</u> very important because knowing <u>why</u> something went wrong is crucial to developing an effective intervention to stop the problem from recurring in the future.

Near-miss reporting programs are as successful as they are because, with some important exceptions, they generally protect the provider of information from being punished based upon the information provided. The theory of the protection is that the best way, and sometimes the only way, to find out about defects in a complex system is from the people who operate the system; but the people who operate the system are obviously reluctant to provide any information that might be used against them. Contrary to popular belief, however, near-miss reporting programs do not provide "get out of jail free" cards to those who submit reports because most programs expressly deny protection for information about intentional or criminal wrongdoing, and many also exclude information about accidents. Significantly, other than with respect to accidents, these denials of protection are generally based upon the <u>intent</u> of the operator (or upon something within the operator's control that affects intent, such as substance abuse), rather than upon the type of event.

Running a red signal significantly increases the likelihood of injury or worse, and train crews are obviously well aware of that. Hence, it is safe to assume that train crews do not run red signals intentionally. Moreover, it was revealed in the public hearing for this accident that, despite various efforts to stop the problem, the rate of running red signals is not generally improving. As a result, two significant questions arise – namely, why are competent, highly trained professionals doing something that they know may cause them harm or worse, and why is this problem so resistant to an effective solution?

In order for the industry to make meaningful progress on the rate of red-signal running, safety and operations experts must know why the problem keeps occurring; and the best source of information about why the problem keeps occurring, and very often the <u>only</u> source of information about why the problem keeps occurring, is the crews who have run signals. Until the information about why red signals are being run is protected by C^3RS, the industry will not have the information it needs to develop and implement effective remedies.

Accordingly, I would urge the FRA and the railroad industry to use the intent of the operator, rather than the nature of the event, to determine eligibility for C^3RS protection, and hence to provide protection to those who report about red-signal running unless there is criminal or intentional wrongdoing. Once the industry begins to find out why red signals are being run, it can begin, finally, to understand this nagging problem enough to develop effective solutions that will help eliminate it.

Chairman Hersman and Members Sumwalt, Rosekind, and Weener joined in this statement.

Member Earl F. Weener, concurring:

I support the accident report concerning the head-on collision of the two Union Pacific Railroad Company freight trains occurring near Goodwell, Oklahoma. Sadly, as we have seen before in other rail accidents, this accident did not need to happen. There were numerous opportunities for intervention prior to the accident; and yet, with likely the best of intentions of helping out a colleague, instead three people lost their lives. From my tenure as an advocate for safety in the corporate environment, non-profit environment and the government environment, I am troubled by this outcome. It begs the question: why is there such disparity in approaches to safety between the railroad industry and other transportation modes?

From a general standpoint, a basic survey of the safety regulatory schemes and industry practices applicable to the various modes clearly indicates the railroad industry, with some exceptions, lags behind the more developed, sophisticated frameworks applied in other transportation modes. For example, as the report documents, with limited exceptions, the medical requirements for the aviation, commercial trucking and marine industries far exceed those of the rail industry both in scope and specificity. As well, in terms of safety concepts such as safety management systems (SMS), crew resource management, and fatigue risk management, other modes appear to be engaged in more aggressive action to mitigate risk, whether through government intervention or by industry initiative. Additionally, from a technology perspective, aviation has made significant strides toward mitigating safety risks through the advancement of technologies such as traffic collision avoidance systems (T-CAS) and terrain awareness and warning systems (TAWS), and commercial vehicles are benefitting from advancements in stability control and collision avoidance technology, yet we see efforts in the rail industry to delay and confound implementation of technology such as positive train control.

In attempting to understand this disparity between the rail industry's approach to safety and other modal approaches I considered both the history and evolution of the various transportation modes, as well as the operational differences between them. However, I have yet to find justification for the diverging views. On the one hand, there is the marine industry, with its time honored history and tradition, which has nonetheless managed to embrace risk management principles and innovation. Alternatively, the relatively young aviation industry often appears to be leading the curve as far as developing and advancing safety concepts and spurring technological advancements. Similarly, all modes of transportation share common operational challenges, although there may be unique characteristics to each mode which require the development of appropriate mitigations to address these challenges. Nonetheless, as demonstrated by implementation of SMS concepts and fatigue risk management programs across modal operations, there is more commonality than distinction among the transportation modes when it comes to advancing safety.

Also, from a business standpoint, safety just makes good sense. As industry leaders from the marine and aviation modes have learned, companies that cannot manage safety are unlikely to manage a profitable company. This maxim takes into account more than costs related to a specific accident; it also involves the costs associated with day-to-day operations such as work force loss or injury, insurance premiums, company reputation, lost productivity, and environmental stewardship. In other words, safety must be managed, just as other functions of a company's operation are managed. In all, development of a sound safety culture, a dedicated approach to safety, leads to cost savings rather than costs on the company's bottom line.

As is often quoted, "safety culture is enlightened self-interest." Candidly, after reviewing accident investigations for the derailment and subsequent hazardous materials fire at Cherry Valley, Illinois; the collision of coal train with a maintenance-of-way equipment train in Red Oak, Iowa; the collision of two freight trains at Two Harbors, Minnesota; and this accident, along with participating in the Board's forum on positive train control, it appears the rail industry could stand some enlightenment.

Vice Chairman Hart and Member Sumwalt joined in this statement.

Appendix: Investigation and Hearing

The NTSB was notified on June 24, 2012, of the collision of two UP trains near Goodwell, Oklahoma. The NTSB launched an investigator-in-charge and eight other investigative team members from its headquarters and from its Los Angeles and Chicago regional offices. Mark R. Rosekind was the NTSB Board Member on scene.

The FRA; the UP; the BLET; the UTU; Electro-Motive Diesel, Inc.; and the Guymon, Oklahoma, Fire Department were parties to the investigation.

An en banc investigative hearing for this accident investigation was held at NTSB headquarters on February 26, 2013. This hearing addressed three broad issues: (1) an overview of the accident, investigation, and the UP's railroad system; (2) the UP's management of human error; and (3) the current status of the UP's PTC implementation. The parties to the hearing were the FRA, the UP, the BLET, and the UTU. The transcript of the hearing proceeding is available in the public docket.

References

Colblinder. 2013. "Online Farnsworth D-15 Colorblindness Test." http://www.colblindor.com/2009/03/10/online-farnsworth-d-15-dichotomous-color-blindness-test/. Accessed April 9, 2013.

Colorblindness. 2013. "Colorblindness: Information: Identification: Solutions. http://www.colour-blindness.com/colour-blindness-tests/ishihara-colour-test-plates/. Accessed April 10, 2013.

FAA (Federal Aviation Administration). 2013. *Guide for Aviation Medical Examiners.* http://www.faa.gov/about/office_org/headquarters_offices/avs/offices/aam/ame/guide/media/guide.pdf. Accessed April 9, 2013.

Federal Register. 2013. Vol. 78, no. 63 (April 2).

----. 2011. Vol. 76, no. 168 (August 30).

----. 2008. Vol. 73, no. 231 (December 1).

FRA (Federal Railroad Administration). 2012. *Railroad Safety: Amtrak Has Made Progress in Implementing Positive Train Control, but Significant Challenges Remain.* Washington, DC: OIG–E–2013–03.

----. 2005. *Medical Standards for Railroad Workers* (Final Report). Washington, DC: DOT/FRA/RRS–05/01.

NHBLI (National Heart, Blood and Lung Institute). "Calculate Your Body Mass Index," accessed June 5, 2013, http://www.nhlbi.nih.gov/guidelines/obesity/BMI/bmicalc.htm.

NIAAA (National Institute on Alcohol Abuse and Alcoholism). 2013. *Alcohol's Effects on the Body.* Accessed February 4, 2013. http://www.niaaa.nih.gov/alcohol-health/alcohols-effects-body.

NTSB (National Transportation Safety Board). 2013a. *CSX Transportation (CSX) Freight Train Strikes Stopped CSX Freight Train Near Mineral Springs, North Carolina, May 24, 2011.* Railroad Accident Brief RAB-13/01. Washington, DC: NTSB.

----. 2013b. *Collision of Two Canadian National Railway Freight Trains near Two Harbors, Minnesota, September 30, 2010.* Railroad Accident Report RAR-13/01. Washington, DC: NTSB.

----. 2013c. *Transcript of Investigative Hearing on Head-on Collision of Two Union Pacific Railroad Company Freight Trains Near Goodwell, Oklahoma, June 24, 2012.* February 26, 2013. Washington, DC: NTSB.

----. 2013d. *Transcript of "Positive Train Control: Is it on Track?" Forum.* February 27, 2013. Washington, DC: NTSB.

----. 2012. *Collision of BNSF Coal Train With the Rear End of Standing BNSF Maintenance-of-Way Equipment Train, Red Oak, Iowa, April 17, 2011.* Railroad Accident Report RAR-12/02. Washington, DC: NTSB.

----. 2010. *Collision of Metrolink Train 111 and Union Pacific Train LOF65-12, Chatsworth, California, September 12, 2008.* Railroad Accident Report RAR-10/01. Washington, DC: NTSB.

----. 2007. *Collision of Two CN Freight Trains, Anding, Mississippi, July 10, 2005.* Railroad Accident Report RAR-07/01. Washington, DC: NTSB.

----. 2002. *Collision of Two Canadian National/Illinois Central Railway Trains Near Clarkston, Michigan, November 15, 2001.* Railroad Accident Report RAR-02/04. Washington, DC: NTSB.

----. 2001. *Collision Involving Three Consolidated Rail Corporation Freight Trains Operating in Fog on a Double Main Track, Near Bryan, Ohio, January 17, 1999.* Railroad Accident Report RAR-01/01. Washington, DC: NTSB.

----. 1999. *Collision of Norfolk Southern Corporation train 255L5 with Consolidated Rail Corporation Train TV 220, Butler, Indiana, March 25, 1998,* Railroad Accident Report RAR-99/02. Washington, DC: NTSB.

----. 1998. *Collision and Derailment of Union Pacific Railroad Freight Trains 5981 North and 9186 South, In Devine, Texas, June 22, 1997.* Railroad Accident Report RAR-98/02. Washington, DC: NTSB.

----. 1997a. *Collision and Derailment of Maryland Rail Commuter MARC Train 286 and National Railroad Passenger Corporation AMTRAK Train 29, Near Silver Spring, Maryland, February 16, 1996.* Railroad Accident Report RAR-97/02. Washington, DC: NTSB.

----. 1997b. *Near Head-On Collision and Derailment of Two New Jersey Transit Commuter Trains Near Secaucus, New Jersey, February 9, 1996.* Railroad Accident Report RAR-97/01. Washington, DC: NTSB.

UP (Union Pacific Railroad). 2010. *General Code of Operating Rules.* Sixth Edition. Omaha, NE: Union Pacific Railroad.